Johannes Bobrowski

Under the Edge of Night

Selected Poems

TRANSLATED FROM THE GERMAN BY

RICHARD SIEBURTH

NYRB/POETS

nyrb NEW YORK REVIEW BOOKS *New York*

THIS IS A NEW YORK REVIEW BOOK
PUBLISHED BY THE NEW YORK REVIEW OF BOOKS
207 East 32nd Street, New York, NY 10016
www.nyrb.com

The translation of this work was supported by a grant from the Goethe-Institut.

The poems in this volume have been selected and translated from Johannes Bobrowski's *Gesammelte Gedichte*, first published in German in 2017 by Deutsche Verlags-Anstalt, a division of Penguin Random House Verlagsgruppe GmbH, München, Germany.

Library of Congress Cataloging-in-Publication Data
Names: Bobrowski, Johannes, 1917–1965 author | Sieburth, Richard translator
Title: Under the edge of night: selected poems of Johannes Bobrowski / Johannes Bobrowski; translated and edited by Richard Sieburth.
Other titles: Under the edge of night (Compilation)
Description: New York: New York Review Books, 2026. | Series: New York Review Books poets
Identifiers: LCCN 2026013846 (print) | LCCN 2026013847 (ebook) | ISBN 9798896230977 paperback | ISBN 9798896230984 ebook
Subjects: LCGFT: Poetry
Classification: LCC PT2603.O13 U53 2026 (print) | LCC PT2603.O13 (ebook)
LC record available at https://lccn.loc.gov/2026013846
LC ebook record available at https://lccn.loc.gov/2026

ISBN 979-8-89623-097-7
Available as an electronic book; ISBN 979-8-89623-098-4

Cover and book design by Emily Singer.

The authorized representative in the EU for product safety and compliance is eucomply OÜ, Pärnu mnt 139b-14, 11317 Tallinn, Estonia, hello@eucompliancepartner.com, +33 757690241.

Printed in the United States of America on acid-free paper.
10 9 8 7 6 5 4 3 2 1

Contents

FROM **UNPUBLISHED POEMS**

INTRODUCTION
Shadowlands

> One must wait
> to draw a night song from these names,
> the then and the now, the dark and light
> as they alternate, just out of reach
>
> —Michael Palmer, "After Hölderlin"

Johannes Bobrowski was born in the last year of the Great War in the Baltic town of Tilsit, the northeasternmost outpost of the German Empire, situated on the river Memel—which, ever since the fifteenth-century Treaty of Melno between the Teutonic Knights and the Polish-Lithuanian alliance, had marked the boundary between the Germanic West and the Slavic East. With the Treaty of Versailles in 1919, however, everything changed: All the maps in the Baltic region needed to be redrawn to accommodate the postwar aspirations of the newly independent states of Latvia, Estonia, Lithuania, and Poland. The former German port of Danzig became a free city administered by the League of Nations. The medieval coastal town of Königsberg, the traditional capital of the Duchy of Prussia, was reassigned to the Weimar Republic as an exclave separated from the rest of Germany by the Polish Corridor. As for the area where Bobrowski grew up around Tilsit, this small frontier region now became known as the Territoire de Memel, a free protectorate of the Entente Cordiale States, to be provisionally administered by the French. Eventually handed back to the fledgling Republic of Lithuania, the heavily German-speaking Memelland enclave would later be forcefully annexed, along with Bohemia and Moravia, by the irredentist Third Reich in the spring of 1939, six months before Hitler's invasion of Poland.

During his childhood and high-school years, Bobrowski often spent his holidays in the Memelland while visiting his grandparents' small holdings in the Lithuanian village of Motzichken on the river Jūra. Like Wordsworth's home in Cockermouth with its river Derwent or Heaney's family farm in the Ulster borderlands of County Derry, the landscape of this enclave, along with its local dialects and folklore, would nurture Bobrowski's versions of pastoral for years to come. Elegiacally looking back on the region in the wake of the ravages inflicted upon it by the Nazis and Soviets during World War II, he would idealize this land of his youth as a kind of lost Arcadia, a multiethnic, multicultural, multilingual, multi-creedal *Heimat* in which Poles, Lithuanians, Latvians, Russians, Germans, Gypsies, and Jews could all live alongside each other in (relative) harmony, sheltered in a parenthesis that belonged neither to the East nor the West.

In 1928, at age eleven, Bobrowski moved to Königsberg, where he would spend his next formative decade. Enrolled in the prestigious Kant Lyceum, he spent his secondary-school years receiving a solid education in the classics (Latin and Greek) and in local philosophy (especially Hamann, the Magus of the North, whose work he revered). Among his extracurricular activities as a typical *Bildungsbürger*: piano and organ lessons, choir practice, music theory and composition, painting. And, above all, poetry: His school notebooks included amateur sonnets, ghazels, hexameters, and distichs alongside imitations of Klopstock, Hölderlin, and Goethe, while his readings in modern German verse tended toward George, Rilke, Trakl, Heym, and Benn—all of whose voices would reemerge in his later work.

As an eastern exclave severed from its German fatherland, Königsberg in the 1920s and '30s was particularly susceptible to the rise of anti-Semitism and revanchist nationalism. The son of a nonconformist Baptist with Huguenot roots, the teenage Bobrowski followed in his father's footsteps in 1934 by joining the Confessing Church (Bekennende Kirche)—a Protestant splinter group inspired by such activist theologians as Karl Barth and Dietrich Bonhoeffer that was politically opposed to the "Aryan clause" by which the Third Reich wanted to ban all converted Jews from participation in the newly established national German Evangelical Church. Throughout his life, Bobrowski would remain a quiet, antinomian Protestant, practicing his faith from the deep wells of his pietistic *Innerlichkeit*—or Inner Emigration, as this private withdrawal from the public sphere came to be called among German intellectuals and artists in the 1930s.

Whatever his personal religious or political convictions, upon his graduation from high school in 1937 Bobrowski enlisted in the army, optimistically hoping to proceed on to his university studies in art history in Berlin after a brief two-year stint. Initially stationed in Königsberg to undergo training as a *Funker* or radio operator, when the war broke out in September 1939 he was summarily re-upped and mobilized as a lance corporal in the Wehrmacht's signal corps, first serving on the Polish front and then, during the invasion of France the following year, posted to the Moselle and the coast of Normandy. With the launching of Operation Barbarossa in the early summer of 1941, he was transferred to a unit stationed on Lake Ilmen, just south of Novgorod, where he would spend the next two years as a telephone communications specialist. While following the brutal advance of the northern *Heeresgruppe* through the Baltic lands, he happened to witness the pogrom that took place in Lithuania's capital of Kaunas—a town he had known from his youth—in which 3,800 Jews were put to death by SS Einsatzgruppen and their local collaborators on a single June day. It would take him until 1958—seventeen years after the fact—to unearth this originary trauma in a stark poem simply entitled "Kaunas 1941."

Installed behind the lines on Lake Ilmen, the young signal corpsman spent his idle hours composing verse, some of which he collected in an unpublished manuscript notebook entitled "Under the Edge of Night" and the remainder of which—a sequence of eight classical odes—appeared in the German literary magazine *Das Innere Reich*. Founded in 1934 as a semiofficial refuge for German writers, many of whom were conservative escapees into the Inner Emigration, its pages featured patriotic hymns by Hölderlin alongside praises for the Nordic sculpture of Arno Breker. Paul Celan would later be dismayed to discover that his colleague Bobrowski had published his first poems in this Third Reich magazine, even though its wartime contributors also included Günter Eich, who would go on to become a founding member of the left-wing postwar West German Gruppe 47 (and to write a poem sarcastically rhyming "Hölderlin" with "urine"), as well as Peter Huchel, later to achieve eminence as the editor of East Germany's most prestigious literary journal, *Sinn und Form*.

Generally overlooked by critics, Bobrowski's wartime juvenilia (omitted from this selection) nonetheless foretell signature features of his later work. Many of the pieces are straightforward landscape poems that rely on the tropes popularized by the interwar "magical realist" *Naturlyrik* of such established figures as Oskar Loerke and Wilhelm Lehmann. Often equipped with toponymic titles derived from the Slavic place-names of the towns through which his regiment had passed, the exotic icons and monasteries he evoked also recall the spiritual pilgrimage through Orthodox Russia recorded in Rilke's 1905 *Das Stunden-Buch* (*The Book of Hours*)—although at their worst these landscapes come off as mere kitschy postcards from the front. The remainder of the poems rehearse a kind of *Trümmerpoesie* (rubble poetry) that in the German tradition hearkened back to the baroque verse composed by Andreas Gryphius amidst the miseries and massacres of the Thirty Years' War. Here Bobrowski's poetry, especially in those odes dealing with the devastated city of Novgorod and the wreckage of its Saint Sophia cathedral, becomes more pointedly allegorical, wearily illustrating the sheer vanity of mortal discord, yet holding out the chiliastic hope that after all this ruination some Second Coming might be at hand.

"The first thing we learned here was seeing," Bobrowski wrote to one of the editors of *Das Innere Reich* in 1943, evidently alluding to that observational *Augenwerk* (working of the eye) that Rilke famously undertook on the advice of Rodin to rid his early poetry of its nebulousness. Yet the young soldier poet went on to admit: "However much we tried to address the landscape, it answered us back with nothing; the difficulty of engaging with the endlessness of the Russian expanses only heightened our sense of being lost, and so we instead turned our eyes upward to the path of the clouds, to the hues of eventide, and to the stars, even though our words could not keep pace with them." Trying to find an idiom for the dread inspired by the infinite incommunicability of the eastern plains, Bobrowski disguises his angst by donning the prosodic straitjacket of Horace's Alcaic Odes. Laboriously stitching his German meters into their quantitative Latin originals—choriambs and all—he very likely thought that the noble garb of these neoclassical quatrains might thereby achieve the marmoreal grandeur of the sublime. Instead, they today merely read as the abandoned museum pieces of Bobrowski's Wehrmacht years—from the debris of which he would have to learn to reconstruct his future work.

Captured near Riga on the last day of the war and (miraculously) taken alive by the Russians, Bobrowski spent his next four and a half years in Soviet POW camps. Upon his return to Berlin in 1949 to rejoin his wife, he wrote an (unpublished) memoir of his prison experiences in central Russia, wherein he described his manual labors as a coal miner and his comradery with his fellow inmates, for whom he put on plays and other entertainments, while occasionally dashing off love poems for them to send home. He also came back with an enormous notebook of verse that he had composed as a POW—largely, so it would seem, just to keep his ear operational and his pen busy. Most of these prison rhymes, though technically quite proficient, rarely surpass the sentimental clichés of traditional German poetastery, and he did well to keep these *Heimatlieder* (as he unfortunately called them) under wraps thereafter.

Having found a comfortable Berlin job in the children's book sector of the GDR's publishing industry, Bobrowski finally returned to serious writing in mid-1952 with the composition of his first major postwar poem, "Pruzzian Elegy." He later claimed that this piece had been inspired by his reading of Huchel's most recent work: Whereas his own earlier wartime verse had been singularly devoid of any human agency other than the poet's uncertain lyric "I," Huchel's (Marxist) georgics now inspired Bobrowski to conceive of landscapes as spaces that were instead profoundly *peopled*, that is, whose topography needed be read in relation to the objective histories of its inhabitants. Ever since his childhood in the Memelland, Bobrowski had been struck by the mysterious and half-hidden story of the enclave, evident in the archaic burial mounds and ruined ramparts that still marked its landscape—silent traces of those ancient indigenous Baltic tribes collectively known as the Old Prussians who had for centuries fished and farmed along its lagoons and rivers until their virtual extermination in the thirteenth century by the Teutonic Knights.

These Knights of Mary, frustrated by their failures in the Holy Land, had been looking for a favorable Crusade—the Spaniards were now driving out the Moors from Córdoba, and the last of the heretical Albigensians had been duly slaughtered in Béziers. Under Polish and papal encouragement, the German Order, clad in its ominous white robes emblazoned with black crosses, decided to venture northeastward into the Baltics to Christianize the last remaining pocket of heathendom in Europe. The Old Prussian warriors put up a valiant resistance, but in the end some eighty thousand autochthones were eradicated between 1230 and 1283 in the name of the Virgin. Acting as settler colonialists, their new masters proceeded to import fresh immigrants from the west while forcing the surviving population to convert to Catholicism and swear allegiance to the German Holy Roman Empire, where many eventually lost their identities. By the early eighteenth century, the language of the Old Prussians had completely disappeared. As Bobrowski later would imagine in his poem "Dead Language," only the birds continued to speak it—like the Latin of the nightingales in the albas of Provençal poetry.

Typically enough, none of this historical epos is made explicit in Bobrowski's "Pruzzian Elegy"—although the two zeds of its title provided a clue to readers that this ancient Baltic people was not to be confused with the later German "Prussians" who, after having exterminated its gods, went on to appropriate its proud ethnonym. Yet any member of his generation would have certainly remembered being taught in school that the Teutonic Knights' heroic conquest of the eastern pagans not only proved the eternal racial and cultural superiority of the Germans over the subaltern Slavs but also justified their ongoing right to expansionist *Lebensraum*. While for the moment eschewing the whole fraught matter of the Holocaust (still an unconscionable excuse for mere poetry, as Adorno had recently insisted), Bobrowski's "Pruzzian Elegy" nonetheless manages to allegorically translate Germany's violent medieval past into an ominous foreshadowing of its recent wartime predations in the East.

In a cascade of dactyls, Bobrowski liturgically laments the extinction of an entire people and its pantheon of nature gods. As he summons up the Old Pruzzian *Volk* from the dead, its monosyllabic note echoes through his lines like a baroque organ pedal point (or, to my American ear, like the anaphora of Whitman):

> Folk
> of the black forests,
> of the surging rivers
> and broad lagoons, seafolk!
> Folk
> of the night hunt,
> of herds and summer fields!
> Folk
> of Perkūns and Peckols,
> of Patrimpas, wreathed with wheat!
> Folk
> like no other, folk of joy,
> like no other, folk of death—

Folk
of smoldering groves
and burning huts and trampled
seedlings and bloodstained streams—
Folk
sacrificed to the singe
of lightning, screams shrouded
in smoke and flame—

This sprawling seventy-six-line threnody would have to wait another three years to finally see print in Huchel's widely read GDR journal *Sinn und Form*—where, sometimes compared to Celan's now-celebrated "Death Fugue" of 1948, it immediately made Bobrowski's reputation. When he later chose this anti-fascist elegy as the centerpiece of his first volume of poetry in 1961, its West German publisher decided to drop the poem altogether, one of its politically correct in-house readers having objected to the Nazi tinge of its (purely anthropological, purely poetical) usage of the word *Volk*. The famous indirectness, or outright hermeticism, of much of Bobrowski's postwar poetry would be his way of slipping under the radar of those various regimes of censorship, be they East or West German, that continued to haunt him throughout his career. Censorship, Borges remarked, is the mother of metaphor.

Around the time that his "Pruzzian Elegy" first appeared in print in 1955, Bobrowski began to envisage a larger, more anthological collection of poems that he proposed to call (with a nod to Goethe's *West-Eastern Divan*) his *Sarmatian Divan*. The Sarmatia of its title alluded to the name given by the Alexandrian geographer Ptolemy to the vast and undefined region that stretched from the Vistula eastward to the Volga and from the Black and Caspian Seas northward to the rims of the Baltic. The ancient cartographer had derived this appellation from the Sarmatians, those legendary equestrian warriors of Iranian origin who (like their cousins the Scythians, ancient Greece's *barbaroi*), had dominated the Eurasian steppes between the fifth century BC and the fourth century AD before their culture was eventually absorbed by the invading Huns and German Goths. An aficionado of genealogy, Bobrowski liked to imagine that his ancient aristocratic Polish Lithuanian ancestors were the descendants of this mythical *Volk*. When asked to define his nationality, he would reply that he was more than just a German with a Polish surname but rather a "Eurasian" whose roots reached back to the immense dreamscape of the Pontic Steppe evoked in his 1956 poem "The Sarmatian Plain":

> Plain,
> giant sleep,
> big with dreams, the spread
> of your sky, a bell tower,
> the larks high up
> in the eaves—
>
> Rivers
> stream round your flanks,
> the damp forest shade, the bright
> unending fields

traversed by all the peoples
following the bird routes
in the early year
of that endless time

you gathered for them
out of the dark. I see you:
the heavy beauty
of that eyeless clay head,
named Ishtar or somebody else,
discovered in the mud.

Those endless eastern plains that had so defeated his eye in wartime Russia here at last come into view, an oneiric motherland alive with the memories of ancient migrations and the buried vestiges of chthonic gods. If you go back far enough in time, Charles Olson once noted, it turns into space—or what Rilke called *Raum*, or sheer room.

Bobrowski would later tear out a page from his old Brockhaus atlas and grid out its map of Central Europe into a series of numbered zones that corresponded to the geographical and historical locations of the poems he wanted to include in his projected *Sarmatian Divan*. Zone 1 encompassed the Königsberg and Memel region of his East Prussian youth; zone 2, the Baltic lands of Lithuania, Latvia, and Estonia; zone 3, western Russia up to the Urals and the Black Sea; zone 4, Poland, Belorussia, and the Ukraine; and zone 5, Danzig to Berlin. Bobrowski of course could not possibly have been aware that these zones also roughly corresponded to what the historian Timothy Snyder has labeled the Bloodlands, where between 1933 and 1945 roughly fourteen million people were mass murdered by the Soviets and the Nazis, but his atlas mappings nonetheless allowed him to chart out the arrangement of the poems he would gather into his first two volumes of verse, *Sarmatian Time* (1961) and *Shadowland Rivers* (1962), both conceived as mythical descents into space-time to rescue the past from oblivion—as in this address to the lost habitus of his childhood:

Village between marsh and river,
raw in the crow-light
of your early winter, the road
through the alders overgrown,
the huts sodden with the stain
of rain and peat smoke, you,
my unending light,
my muted light,
scrawled upon the edges
of my life, archaic light:

Image of a hunter, animal-
headed, engaged in magic,
painted on the rock
of an icy cave.

Published back-to-back, the 150-odd pages of Bobrowski's first two books present themselves as a single protracted verse sequence or poetic cycle—although their historical sweep also bears a family (if not formal) resemblance to other such modernist epics as Pound's *Cantos*, Williams's *Paterson*, or Olson's *Maximus Poems*. The first volume, *Sarmatian Time*, is divided into four sonata-like movements, the first of which, centered around the historic Lithuanian capital of Vilna (or Vilnius) and its river Vilia, resurrects the poet's memories of the doomed landscapes of his youth—an era without any specific private stories to admit (unlike Wordsworth), yet sustained by the rush of remembered sensoria and images. The second movement is entirely taken up by the long lament of his "Pruzzian Elegy," while the third introduces a sequence of more sprightly *Personengedichte* (persona poems) devoted to the vitae of such exiles and outcasts as François Villon, Luis de Gongóra, Dylan Thomas, and Joseph Conrad (a distant Polish relative of Bobrowski's). In its final section, the book delves back into the Russian otherworld where, amid the ruins of Novgorod and its nearby Lake Ilmen, the bard sings of his wartime *Winterreise* through the glacial solitudes of the east and its great Hölderlinian rivers.

The ensuing volume, *Shadowland Rivers*, more loosely structured into three parts, further pursues this path of mourning and rememoration along the various stations of the poet's private Sarmatia. But as its title indicates, these lands have now notably darkened into a domain of shadows—a territory of restless, unappeased shades who have wandered forth from the hell of the past to haunt the poet's consciousness:

> Open up,
> I can't make it through,
> all your dead so
> unruly in me.

The ghostly Jews of Lithuania had made their initial appearances in Bobrowski's verse of the early 1950s, which included vignettes of itinerant peddlers, horse traders, bearded Hassidim, and the community of the faithful in Vilna (known as the Jerusalem of the North, ninety percent of whose large Jewish population disappeared in World War II), alongside Chagall's evocations of vanished shtetl life in Galicia. But it would take the trauma so belatedly relived in his poem "Kaunas 1941" to make Bobrowski fully confront his own implication in the atrocities committed by "the slavering wolves" of the SS as they hunted down the local Jews before his very eyes. Its memorable last line—deeply Lutheran in its penitential despair—simply reads: "My dark is already come."

Further Jewish-themed poems appeared in *Shadowland Rivers*: "Elder Blossom," based on Isaac Babel's autobiographical memory of a 1905 pogrom in Odessa, and "Report," a documentary account of a 1939 photo Bobrowski had recently come across, in which a certain Bajla Gelblung, recently escaped from the Warsaw ghetto to join the partisan resistance, stands there young and defiant in a Polish uniform, surrounded by her smug German captors. But abandoning these various attempts to capture the fate of the Jews in cameo form, Bobrowski went on to compose a sequence of anguished poems directly addressed to the poets Gertude Kolmar, Else Laske-Schüler, and Nelly Sachs—all Jewish, all victims of the Nazis. To Kolmar, murdered at Auschwitz in 1943, he confessed his ongoing inability to cast the horror into words:

But the dark times
have not died, my speech
strays, all
rusted up with blood.

To Laske-Schüler, who had died in 1945 after fleeing Germany for Jerusalem, he numbly rehearsed the forgotten Polish place-names of Jewish deportation and extermination, while indirectly invoking the solace of the book of Daniel:

Przemysł, Brzozów, whosoever
dug his own grave
now lies in it,
sprawled. In Mielec
the house of God
on fire, above the flames
a voice, the voice
of hundreds of mouths,
arising
from suffocation. How say
this: out of the furnaces
emerged praise
of God—how say
this?

I no longer
know.

To Nelly Sachs, who had escaped to Sweden in 1940 a week before she was scheduled to report to a concentration camp,

Bobrowski offered this biblical ray of hope to the survivors of the Shoah:

> Who has a place
> to lay his head, shall
> sleep, shall hear
> in his dreams a cry
> soaring over the plains
> and waters—and there was light,
> parting the two hills,
> the paths, stones, riverbanks
> recognizable, glints of green...

He closed the poem by quoting a fragile image of salvation rescued from one of Sachs's own verses: "Dandelion seeds, // yet winged with prayer."

"To Nelly Sachs" was Bobrowski's response to a poem that Celan had dedicated to her the previous year in commemoration of their brief meeting in 1960 in Zurich, where both had experienced an epiphany upon seeing the golden light stream across the Swiss lake on Ascension Day. In a letter to a friend, Celan reported that this (deceptive?) light over the waters had led them to discuss their respective religious beliefs: "May I tell you what she said to me a few days ago—we were speaking about her [Jewish] faith—when I told her about my hope to be able to blaspheme and quarrel with God to the very end? Nelly Sachs merely nodded and commented: *We just don't know what counts...*" Celan's poem, "Zurich, at the Stork Inn," reads in part:

There was talk of your God, I spoke
against him, I
let the heart I had
hope:
for his highest, his death-rattled, his
contending word—

Your eye looked at me, looked away,
your mouth
spoke across to the eye, I heard:

We
just don't know, you know,
we
just don't know,
what counts.

(translated by Pierre Joris)

Celan's and Bobrowski's poems were eventually published side by side in a Suhrkamp Festschrift for Sachs. In this dialogue between the two exiled Holocaust survivors, Celan figures as the tormented atheist who continues to inveigh against the God who abandoned his people, while Sachs is prepared to remain open to his ongoing enigma. Interpreting her airborne dandelion seeds as tiny harbingers of redemption, Bobrowski quietly sides with Sachs.

Bobrowski had been closely following Celan's poetry ever since the early 1950s. The two eventually entered into correspondence after Celan sent Bobrowski his translations of

Mandelstam from Paris in 1959—which the still relatively unpublished Bobrowski gratefully took as a significant consecration by a major poet and (so he thought) an indirect acknowledgment that, as Celan would later quote Marina Tsvetayeva, "all poets are Jews." But when he received Celan's most recent volume of verse, *Sprachgitter* (*Speechgrille*), that same year, he reacted with considerable ambivalence, comparing the poet's current work to "a perfume factory that once delivered violets but now only deals in desiccated pieces of bark." Too "undynamic," too "ascetic," too "sterile," too "distilled," and impossible to read aloud, these poems seemed to him merely devised to provide "specialized hospital apparatuses for invalids"—though he nonetheless had to confess, belonging as he did to the "vile" German race, that there was no way he could possibly arrive at any objective assessment of the immense sufferings that Celan had faced as a Jew. Bobrowski's reactions reveal, above and beyond their sheer anxiety of influence, his aversion to what he took to be both Celan's nihilism and his fundamental animus against the German language—whose contamination by the Nazis Celan would seek to cleanse and erase in the ever more abstruse idiolect of his later work. By comparison, Bobrowski here emerges as the far more traditional poet, eager to preserve the more lasting legacy of German verse—the baroque poets, Klopstock, Hölderlin, the Romantics, the expressionists—from the rubble of Germany's Zero Hour in 1945. What thou lovest well remains...

He was particularly disturbed by one of Celan's recent lines in *Speechgrille*, "A word—you know: a corpse," which only confirmed his suspicion of Celan's necrophile (and suicidal) obsession with everything dead or inorganic. In "Reawakening," a 1964 poem privately dedicated to Celan upon receipt of a copy of his latest volume, *Die Niemandsrose* (*The No-One's Rose*), Bobrowski took on the mantle of Ezekiel to prophesy that the Valley of Death (or the burial pits of the mass-murdered Jews, "white / with bones, ribs, vertebrae, / radii, lime") would in the fullness of time be healed by the metamorphic power of the Word, especially when attuned to the seasonal regenerations of the green world of Nature—the requisite consolation offered at the close of traditional elegy:

> Go count
> the grass blades,
> go number
> the rainwater threads
> of light, go count
> the tiny leaves and sketch in
> your footsteps, spoors
> of voice and deer,
> and with words
> revive
> the blood
> in lungs and trees,
> and from the walls and stairs
> rid yourselves
> of the rust still stuck
> to your hands, waiting
> to eat at your nails.

It's not time to ask.
It's time for water to flow
around stalks, for a new
dispensation of leaves, for eyes
to be opened by the green.

Among the increasing number of his poems that began appearing in West German magazines and anthologies around 1960, Bobrowski submitted eight of his "Jewish" poems to a small Bavarian press volume tortuously entitled "Tears on the Barbed Wire: Philosemitic Poems by Non-Jewish Authors." Bobrowski always detested the term "philosemitic," tending as it did to merely caricature the Jews into stereotypical victims (or admirable sages à la Lessing's *Nathan the Wise*), while at the same time trivializing Christianity's profound Judaic ancestry. In a letter to Celan, Bobrowski quoted Pascal's celebrated "Memorial" (found in the lining of his coat after his death) to underscore their common heritage: "GOD of Abraham, GOD of Isaac, GOD of Jacob, GOD of Jesus Christ, Your GOD shall be my GOD." Reared in a family of fundamentalist Protestants, upon his postwar return to Berlin Bobrowski continued to regularly attend services at his local Evangelical church, participating in its choir and occasionally playing the organ—whose baroque pulse animates the prosody of so many of his poems. In 1960, he joined the Christian Democratic Union (CDU), the surviving East German faction of the Confessing Church of his youth and the sole semiofficial "bloc party" that represented the minority Christian-humanist opposition to the institutionalized atheism of the Communist regime. Sub rosa, Bobrowski would always remain a deeply Christian poet, devout in his (sometimes rattled) *Innerlichkeit*, yet never explicitly devotional.

Given his membership in the CDU (which also funded the Union Verlag publishing house where he worked as a literary editor), Bobrowski was invited to address Berlin's Evangelical Academy in 1962 with a lecture entitled "Benannte Schuld=Gebannte Schuld?" ("Named Guilt=Managed Guilt?") in which he wondered whether it was enough for Germany simply to make explicit its past sins in order to be rid of them. Taking a page from Martin Buber's influential 1957 essay "On Guilt," Bobrowski argued that the culpability he intended was not just some vague internal or subjective form of neurosis (as Freud or Melanie Klein would have it) but rather something far more existential and far more historical—the result of a deliberate and vicious disruption of the order of sane humane relations between the Germans and their Jewish or Eastern European victims. To name this violence in all its specifics—to do away with the silence or euphemism that engulfed it—was merely the first step in the process of healing. True remembrance or true reparation of the damage would have to depend on reinstituting a genuine I-Thou (instead of an I-It) relation to the Jews or Slavs in order (as Saint Paul put it) to at last come face-to-face with the other. Bobrowski remained vague about the role literature might play in instituting this ethical duty of address, yet virtually every poem he ever wrote implicitly responds to this demand through its repeated rituals of apostrophe—in which an "I" (ever the signal corpsman) dials up or radios a "you" and then awaits an answer from afar to confirm (whatever the intervening static) that some sort of line of communication has been established. As Jonathan Culler has observed, invocation is the very figure of the poet's vocation. In Bobrowski's poetry, apostrophe—like its related verbal mood, the imperative—always initiates an act of welcoming, an extension of hospitality to the *xenos*, or in German, to the *Fremder* (the stranger, the foreigner, the alien). The very first poem of *Sarmatian Time* closes with this exhortation—and this warning: "Welcome in the strangers. / You shall be a stranger. Soon."

Bobrowski's meditations on guilt and hospitality were not the sort of thing the East German authorities were eager to hear. When it came to *Vergangenheitsbewältigung* (coping with the past), the official GDR Cold War line was that the responsibility for the Holocaust lay entirely with the Nazi-infested Federal Republic of Germany, the true successor to the untrammeled capitalism of the Third Reich. If Jews had died, it was not as objects of systematic anti-Semitism but rather as the political and working-class victims of fascism. Like many of the Eastern Bloc countries, the GDR refused to recognize the state of Israel, considering it to be a mere Zionist outpost of Western imperialism, and instead threw its support to the Palestinian independence movement. There was therefore no question of making reparations or of officially apologizing to the Jews as West Germany had done: If their sufferings were to be memorialized, it was only as fellow fighters against Nazism, exploited and sacrificed in order to pave the way for the triumph of the new Communist world order.

Given Bobrowski's growing reputation as a poet in the West, the GDR's Ministry of Culture nonetheless made the unusual decision to accord him permission to bring out his first volume of verse in 1960 with the Stuttgart-based Deutsche

Verlags-Anstalt—the publishers of Celan and Sachs—in tandem with an East German edition by the Union Verlag. Unlike his friend and colleague Huchel, who was dismissed from his overly Western-leaning editorship of *Sinn und Form* in 1962 and placed under house arrest, Bobrowski was now allowed the freedom to travel abroad as a token (and presumably harmless) representative of "dissident" East German literature. Well received at the Gruppe 47's meetings and awarded its annual prize in 1962, he also made appearances at the Frankfurt Book Fair and at the gathering of the Hölderlin Society in Tübingen. In 1964, he traveled to international literary conferences in Finland (where he ran into James Baldwin) and Sweden (where he finally met his idol, Sachs). During these years, reluctantly playing the role of a forty-year-old smiling public man, Bobrowski continued to give lectures, attend symposia, and receive awards—all the while working on his satirical historical novel, *Levin's Mill* (another tale of East Prussian malfeasance against the Jews), for which he received East Germany's most prestigious honor, the Heinrich Mann Prize, in 1964, just six months before he died of undiagnosed appendicitis. His career as a recognized writer, launched by the 1955 appearance of his "Pruzzian Elegy," had barely lasted a decade, yet toward the end, depressed and overworked, drinking heavily, he could barely take it anymore:

Speech
harried
mouth worn out
on the endless path
to the neighbor's house

Bobrowski's third book of verse, *Weathersigns*, appeared in late 1966, two years after his death. Whereas his two previous volumes had been mostly written over the course of the 1950s, this final collection was prepared for publication during the final four years of his life. By mid-1961, he had given up on the dream of his *Sarmatian Divan*: The great "encyclopedic" mosaic he had intended to construct, he now realized, remained out of reach, leaving behind only a provisional scatter of tesserae that still needed to be fitted into a final whole. He was apparently also stung by the mixed reactions to his recent readings of his poems in West Germany, which the younger, more urbane members of the audience (unfairly) described as mere nostalgic *Heimat* verse, too "mossy" in its old-fashioned Eastern Bloc regionalism. It was therefore time, he decided, to move into new, more unexplored directions. He had long complained about the GDR's hostility to any contemporary poetry that did not hew to the pieties of socialist realism. When he began writing in the 1950s, its official verse culture was still dominated by two major voices—Johannes Becher, who spoke for the regime, and Bertolt Brecht, who spoke from both sides of his mouth. Therefore forced to look beyond the GDR for inspiration, Bobrowski instructed himself (often in translation) in the international tradition of the new: the other Germans (Celan, Sachs, Bachmann, Enzensberger), the French (Baudelaire, Rimbaud, Reverdy, Éluard, Perse), the Italians (Montale, Ungaretti), the Spanish speakers (García Lorca, Neruda), the Scandinavians (Tranströmer, Haavikko), the Poles (Herbert, Rozewicz, but not the anti-Communist Miłosz), and of course the Russians—Mandelstam (in Celan's translation) and Pasternak (whom he would later translate himself). His acquaintance with English-language poetry remained relatively meager: Keats, Shelley, Browning, Yeats, Dylan Thomas, and on the American side, the more predictably popular Frost, Sandburg, Masters, Hughes, and, surprisingly, Pound.

Although the impress of thesc foreign readings can already be felt in his earlier verse, their presence becomes more pronounced in the harder-edged brevities of his '60s poetry, whose hermetic late style was what drew me to Bobrowski's work in the first place. Jettisoning the topographical-historical architectonics of his first two volumes together with the long looping rhythms of their Hölderlinian odes, he now decided to devise a book that would read as the terse chronological record of his private and public poetic humors, its manuscripts carefully dated in diaristic fashion. The volume opens under the sign of music with a portrait of the young Bach traveling to Lübeck to inherit the scores of the aging Buxtehude in a ritual passing of the flame. In his previous volumes, Bobrowski had increasingly explored the genre of the *Personengedicht* (which he rediscovered via Benn) with poems spoken in the personae of such precursor figures as Hamann, Hölderlin, and Mickiewicz, and his later work includes portraits of himself as Rabelais, Mozart, and Rosa Luxemburg—or even as the damaged Baltic playwright Lenz. Engaged as he now was in the composition of prose fictions, Bobrowski's clipped character sketches owe much to his apprenticeship to minimalist narratives of his two favorite stylists: Isaac Babel and Robert Walser.

His work in the medium of prose also urged the sentences of his late verse into a new certainty of phrase. Abandoning the often involuted and mannered (Klopstockian) syntax of his earlier poetry, he was now ready to engage in that "direct treatment of the 'thing,' whether subjective or objective" recommended by the imagist Pound:

> The summer is cold, the light
> luffs like a sail, and the fish
> tracks down shadows
> with its fins.

Or this, to Cavafy,:

> Who never saw you shield your eyes
> with your hand as you shrugged your shoulders
> now heard your strophe
> the black of the Attic vase
> the Euphronios figure in red

Occasionally he slips into the mild surrealism of an Éluard:

> The sky's white. A tree
> of birdcalls
> opens its eyes.

Or into the baroque extravagance he so admired in Góngora:

> There lay the Baptist's head,
> at its fractured skull,
> at its ragged hair
> clawed a hand
> with loose bluish nails.

These bursts of phanopoeia lit his way back to the classical tradition of epigram. His late poem "With the Songs of Sappho" collages fragments of her verse with the legend of Solon, the Greek lawgiver who, upon listening to his nephew singing a Sapphic song, asked the boy to teach it to him, "so that I may learn it and die." Bobrowski laconically registers this existential moment of conversion:

Solon
before the house,
in the circling wind:
Sing it again, he says,

that I might learn more
of island cries, their call
so thick upon the earth
in the scorch of weeds,

that I might learn
I too could die of this
same rush of song,
winds at my back,
words at my throat.

While revisiting the shards of Greek and Latin antiquity, Bobrowski's *Spätstil* also ventures into the archaic domain of biblical prophecy: Jonah warning Ninevah of its impending doom, Daniel reading the writing on the wall, Ezekiel proclaiming the restoration of Israel. In "Esther," he takes on the words of the queen imploring her king to save the Jews of Persia from eradication:

If I perish, so
let me perish, I took fright,
your glory hunts the skies
like lightning,
the leaping blood
of trumpets
builds my house.

"You speak, O foreign voice— / with a foreign ear I hear you"—thus Bobrowski's cryptic summation of these late encounters with the voices near and far abroad.

As for what was happening before his eyes in East Berlin between 1961 and 1965, he remained more reticent, choosing (like many another) to adopt an Aesopian *Sklavensprache* (slave language) to trick the ears of the master. One of his late poems begins:

Across the angled sky
Saturn plods
through the shadows,
whistling to his moons.

And ends:

Tomorrow, go strew
ashes over the sky

as Saturn's steps
grow near.

Only the private dating of the manuscript reveals that this poem was written on August 14, 1961, one day after construction on the Berlin Wall had begun. From his offices at the Union Verlag across from Checkpoint Charlie, he witnessed the death of a young *Mauerspringer*, shot while trapped in the barbed wire as he was trying to escape to the other side. Bobrowski destroyed his initial account of this event and rewrote it into a gnomic poem whose horrific occasion has been completely elided:

Here
the bricks and painted walls
lie exposed, the stairway buckles
and the legion of rats
raises its standards—
pigeon corpses.

Similarly, his lines on the death of Pasternak were deceptively entitled "In Memory of B.L." to hide the identity of its subject—still a persona non grata in the GDR, having been forced by the Soviets to decline his Nobel Prize in 1958. A poem about Huchel's 1962 house arrest named no names but simply evoked an anonymous figure who had been forced into silence "by all the sand crammed / down his throat." Aware of the Stasi's ongoing surveillance of his fellow poet, Bobrowski's tone grew ever more paranoid in the months before his death:

Who lurks
behind doors, listening:
A knock
in the attic?

A scene that might have been lifted from the film *The Life of Others*. In a late fragment found in one of his notebooks, he simply noted: "Someone is following you— / Yet you don't turn around."

Despite the somber post–Berlin Wall setting of his final volume, he continued to produce the kind of wry and ludic love poems that had so set his early lyrics apart from the drabness of postwar East German verse. Here too he ran afoul of the official GDR censors who deemed love poetry to be a mere petty bourgeois indulgence in the fantasies of privatized desire. In his own defense, Bobrowski argued that the I-Thou interpellations of love (*agape*) instead established the very ground on which any future utopian socialist community would have to be founded. Set against the shadowlands of postwar Eastern Europe—its human landscapes still haunted by the ghostly presences of countless refugees and deportees—his late poem "Bird Nest" issues a spousal salute to the frail hope of home, built twig by twig, and spoken in the voice of a dove:

My sky
changes with yours,
even as my dove
now over-
flies yours,

I see two shadows
converge
in the oat field.

We trade
eyes,
we pitch
camp:
rain,
like a tale
we tell
half sentences
of green,
I hear:

Approaching my brow
with birdcall
your mouth
bears
feathers and twigs.

NOTE

The German texts of this edition are based on those given in Eberhard Haufe's *Gesammelte Gedichte* (Deutsche Verlags-Anstalt, 2017). My notes have been enriched by Haufe's commentaries on the poems in *Erläuterungen* (Deutsche Verlags-Anstalt, 1998). Biographical background was provided by *Johannes Bobrowski, oder Landschaft mit Leuten* (Marbach, 1994). I also consulted Ruth and Matthew Mead's early UK versions of Bobrowski's verse (*Shadow Lands*, Anvil Press, 1984)—useful as sight-readings but offering little to the ear. Louis Zukofsky defined his poetics as "An integral / Lower limit speech / Upper limit music." Guided by my earlier work on Hölderlin, I have in these translations tried to honor this integral, this ∫, this continuous analog of a sum.

This book is for Christopher Benfey, a necessary angel from the start.

—Richard Sieburth

FROM

Sarmatian Time (1961)

Sarmatische Zeit

1.
Anruf

Wilna, Eiche
du—
meine Birke,
Nowgorod—
einst in Wäldern aufflog
meiner Frühlinge Schrei, meiner Tage
Schritt erscholl überm Fluß.

Ach, es ist der helle
Glanz, das Sommergestirn,
fortgeschenkt, am Feuer
hockt der Märchenerzähler,
die nachtlang ihm lauschten, die Jungen
zogen davon.

Einsam wird er singen:
Über die Steppe
fahren Wölfe, der Jäger
fand ein gelbes Gestein,
aufbrannt' es im Mondlicht.—

Heiliges schwimmt,
ein Fisch,
durch die alten Täler, die waldigen
Täler noch, der Väter
Rede tönt noch herauf:
Heiß willkommen die Fremden.
Du wirst ein Fremder sein. Bald.

1.
Call

Vilna, you
oak—
Novgorod,
my birch—
from the woods my springtime cry
once soared, step by step my days
rang out over the river.

Ah, the summer starlight
has been squandered, the teller
of tales sits hunched
over the fire, those youths
who listened to him all night long
now departed.

He shall sing in solitude:
of the wolves who roam
the steppes, of the hunter
who found a yellow stone
aflare in the moonlight.

Sacred
any fish
that swims through the ancient
valleys, their woods still echoing
the fathers' words:
Welcome in the strangers.
You shall be a stranger. Soon.

(September 25, 1957)

Dorf

Noch die Fremde
wie Pauken, fern.
Ich komm einen Weg.
Unter der Feldbirke draußen
der Hirt, im Laubgeräusch, einer Wolke
Regenlaut. Gegen Abend
ein Lied aus langen Tönen,
ein stilles Geschrei
bei den Büschen.

Dorf, zwischen Moor und dem Strom,
rauh, deiner frühen Winter
Krähenlicht, um die Erlen
der Weg, der verwuchs, die Hütten,
weich, die der Torfrauch
färbte und Regen, du
mein unendliches Licht,
mein glanzloses Licht,
an die Ränder geschrieben
meinem Leben, du Altes:

Bild des Jägers, zaubernd,
tierhäuptig,
gemalt in die eisige
Höhlung, im Fels.

Village

Foreign parts, once
again, like drums, distant,
I come down the road. Out there
in the field, beneath a birch tree,
a shepherd amid the rustling leaves,
a cloud-blast of rain. Toward evening
a song's drawn-out notes,
near the bushes,
muffled cries.

Village between marsh and river,
raw in the crow-light
of your early winter, the road
through the alders overgrown,
the huts sodden with the stain
of rain and peat smoke, you,
my unending light,
my muted light,
scrawled upon the edges
of my life, archaic light:

Image of a hunter, animal-
headed, engaged in magic,
painted on the rock
of an icy cave.

(June 22, 1956)

Kindheit

Da hab ich
den Pirol geliebt—
das Glockenklingen, droben
aufscholls, niedersanks
durch das Laubgehäus,

wenn wir hockten am Waldrand,
auf einen Grashalm reihten
rote Beeren; mit seinem
Wägelchen zog der graue
Jude vorbei.

Mittags dann in der Erlen
Schwarzschatten standen die Tiere,
peitschten zornigen Schwanzschlags
die Fliegen davon.

Dann fiel die strömende, breite
Regenflut aus dem offenen
Himmel; nach allem Dunkel
schmeckten die Tropfen,
wie Erde.

Oder die Burschen kamen
den Uferpfad her mit den Pferden,
auf den glänzenden braunen
Rücken ritten sie lachend
über die Tiefe.

Hinter dem Zaun
wölkte Bienengetön.

Childhood

When I was mad
about orioles,
when the church bells rose
skyward and fell back
among the trellised leaves,

when we squatted at the edge
of the woods, stringing red berries
onto blades of grass, in his cart,
passing by,
the gray Jew.

Back then, the cattle huddled
in the alder's black shade at noon,
flicking away the flies
with angry swats of their tails.

Back then the skies opened,
releasing a mighty
deluge: after all that darkness,
the raindrops tasted
of earth.

Or the young fellows on horseback
along the towpaths, the lathered
sheen of the withers, bay,
as they rode along, laughing
over the deeps.

Behind the fence,
a cloud of buzzing bees.

Später, durchs Dornicht am Schilfsee,
fuhr die Silberrassel
der Angst.
Es verwuchs, eine Hecke,
Düsternis Fenster und Tür.

Da sang die Alte in ihrer
duftenden Kammer. Die Lampe
summte. Es traten die Männer
herein, sie riefen den Hunden
über die Schulter zu.

Nacht, lang verzweigt im Schweigen—
Zeit, entgleitender, bittrer
von Vers zu Vers während:
Kindheit—
da hab ich den Pirol geliebt—

Later, the silver rattle
of fear among the thornbushes
by a lake choked with reeds.
The hedge, long untended,
darkening window and door.

Back then the old woman would sing
in her sweet-smelling chamber. The lantern
sputtered in tune. Men stepped
into the room, calling out to their dogs
over their shoulders.

Night, forever branching off into silence—
Time's bitter lapse
from one line to the next:
Childhood—
when I was mad about orioles.

(November 14, 1956)

Nymphe

Zeit der Zikaden, weiße
Zeit, als der Junge am Wasser
saß, die runde Stirn
auf die Arme senkte. Wohin
ist er gegangen?

Wege sind
durch den Wald,
verborgne. Da hol ich ein blutendes
Kraut. Auf die Steine leg ichs,
ruf hinterm Rain den jagenden
Häherschrei, hell.

Und ergrünenden Blicks
taucht sie im stäubenden, weichen
Erlenschatten herauf.
Syrinx, dein Ach, ein Geklirr,
fährt durch die Büsche.

Nymph

Cicada season, white
season, when the boy sat
by the water, resting his forehead
on his arms. Where
has he gone?

There are ways
through the woods,
hidden ways. There I gather a bleeding
herb. I lay it upon the stones.
At field's edge, I mimic
the bright jeer of the jay.

And, eyes gone green,
it darts into the sifted
alder shade. Syrinx,
your cry of fright,
a rustle in the reeds.

(July 1955)

Fischerhafen

Abends
ehe die Boote fort
treiben, eins um das andre,
da lieb ich dich.

Bis an den Morgen
lieb ich dich mit dem Stroh in der Kammer,
mit dem Landwind über dem Dach,
mit der Hecke vor deinem Haus,
mit dem Hundegebell
ehe es hell wird.

Das Gesicht voll Fischdunst, im Tau
werd ich kommen: einer,
der seiner Hände
Wärme vertut an die Silbergestalt
Nacht. Salzigen Munds
kommt er. Jetzt
springt er ins letzte Boot.

Fishing Port

Evenings,
before the boats cast off
one after the other,
I love you.

Until morning
I love you in the hayloft,
with the wind of the plains over the roof,
with the hedge in front of your house,
with the dogs barking
before daybreak.

With fish stink on my face
I shall come to you in the dew
like one who wipes the sweat
of his palms on the silver shape
of night. Here he comes
with his salty mouth. And now
leaps into the last boat.

(August 4, 1958)

Auf den jüdischen Händler A.S.

Ich bin aus Rasainen.
Das ist, wo die zweite Waldnacht
vorbeigeht, wenn du vom Strom kommst,
wo die Gehölze sich auftun
und aus den Wiesen drängt
gilbender Sand.

Dort sind die Nächte hell.
Unsre Frauen löschen die Feuer
zeitig. Lang
atmen wir, tief mit dem dunklen
schweifenden Windhauch.

Alles haben wir, jede
Zeit aus den Händen der Väter.
Ihre Sorg' hält uns wach.
Ihr übersterntes Gefürcht
glänzt im Gezweig unsrer Rede.
Frierend schütten wir ihnen
Gräber. Es lagern die Wolken
lange darüber, Rauch.

Immer geht einer davon,
schaut nicht zurück, kein Winken
folgt ihm. Doch hält ihn der Alten
Spruch an den Pfosten des Tores
über dem Meer noch. Fern
weckt ihn der Birkenwege
wehe tönendes Saitenspiel.

To the Jewish Peddler A.S.

I'm from Raseiniai.
Which is two nights into the forest
when you're coming from the river,
where the woods begin to thin out
and the yellow sands seep
into the meadows.

Out there the nights are bright.
Our women are quick
to snuff out the fires. We take a long
deep breath of the dark
wavers of wind.

Everything we possess has always
come from the hands of our fathers.
We are kept awake by their care.
Everything they feared, illuminated by the stars,
brightens the branches of our speech.
Freezing, we shovel them
their graves. Over which
the clouds lie in wait. Smoke.

One of them is always leaving,
not looking back, ungreeted by any
goodbye wave. Yet the wisdom
of the ancients on the doorposts
still bears him overseas. There
to awaken on birch-lined roads
to the woeful strains of harps.

(June 1954)

Die alte Heerstraße

Seitab ist gezogen
auf der verfallenen Straße
der Korse, ein südlicher Kaiser,
winzig vor Zorn, in der Krähen
Spur auf dem Schnee,—
eingeholt von heiligen
Flüchen abends. Die hungernden
Wölfe schleiften Nächte
aus Moordunst ihm nach.

Doch der verblauende Herbst
fährt um das Dorf und die Wolke
auf. Wie Weinen ist eure
Schönheit, Pfade der Heimat, nun.
Sandige Pfade, es schritten
die Jahre euch ab.

Jahre, windbrüchige Winter,
da wir erlauschten das Licht,
singend über dem Feuer,
lehnten schwer am Gestein
Finsternis, auszuschaun
nach tanzenden Inseln des Südmeers.

Und wir dürsten.
So ist dein
Herz ein Brunnen geworden
uns, im Saft der Birken
duftend, im farnigen, goldnen
Nest deiner Schlangen,
Heimat. So sind zu lieben

The Ancient Army Route

He veered sideways
from the route, fallen into
disrepair, this Corsican,
this southern emperor,
tiny with rage, in the crow
tracks on the snow, caught up
in the holy scourge of dusk. Hungry
wolves dragged nights of marsh mist
in his wake.

Yet the autumn blue
spans village and cloud.
Paths of home, your beauty
is now like tears.
Sandy paths, tamped down
by years.

Years, winters brittle with wind,
when we listened to the light
sing over the fire,
when we leaned hard into the rock
of the dark, on the lookout for those isles
that dance upon the southern seas.

And we're dying of thirst.
Thus your heart, O homeland,
has become a fountain
to us, its scent caught
in the sap of birches,
in the golden ferns
of your nested snakes.

deine Söhne gekommen
schattigen Auges immer
von fremden Tischen zurück.—

Einst,
vor Zeiten ist Orpheus
hier gegangen am Hang
dunkel. Es tönt herüber
der Wald seine Klagen ewig.

Ach, den Singenden narrte
die Erde, die zahllose Stimme
Eurydikes, aus Schluchten
her, von Gewässern. Sie beugt den
Rücken uns tiefer, ins stäubende
Kraut, eh mit Schauern, mit zornigen
Regen ausfährt das Jahr.

Thus your sons, their eyes
now shaded, have always returned
from foreign feasts to discover love.

Time was
Orpheus here made his way
down the dark slope
while the woods echoed
his long lament.

Alas, the singer was deceived
by the earth, by many-voiced
Eurydice singing forth from ravine
and stream. She backs us
deeper into the dusty
weeds, before the year departs
in a furious shower of rain.

(October 27, 1955)

Wagenfahrt

Schöner Mond von Mariampol! Auf deinem
strohernen Rand, mein Städtchen,
hinter den Buden
kommt er herauf,
schwer, und hängt ein wenig
nach unten durch. So geht der
Pferdehändler, er kauft
seiner Mutter ein Fransentuch.

Abends
spät
sangen die beiden. Wir fuhren
über den Fluß nach Haus,
an der Fähre mit Ruf und Zuruf
ging Gerede wie Wasser
leicht—und wir hörten ihn lang
über der Stadt,
droben in Türmen, hörten
den jüdischen Mond. Der ist
wie im Gartenwinkel das kleine
Kraut aus Tränen und Küssen,
Raute, unsere Mädchen
brechen es ab.

—

Joneleit, komm, verlier dein
Tuch nicht. Die Alten schlafen.
Ausgesungen wieder
ist eine Nacht.

Wagon Trip

O moon over Mariampol! On your
frazzled hem, my little town,
behind your market stalls, the moon
rises heavy,
hangs there,
and sags back down. Thus
the horse trader on his route, buying
his mother a tasseled shawl.

Late
in the evening,
both were singing. We drove
home across the river,
call and response
at the ferry, the talk
flowing back and forth
light as water, and we heard it
slowly float over the town,
up there in the towers, heard
the Jewish moon, there in the corner
of the garden, a bit of rue,
herb of tears and kisses
plucked by our girls.

——

Yoneleit, come, don't forget
your shawl. The old folks are asleep.
Another night
sung to its end.

(September 3, 1957)

Das Holzhaus über der Wilia

Flußwald,
Dunkel aus Eulengeschrei, in der Grillen
moosweißem Lied, wir sahn
einst das Haus auf dem Ufer,
grau im Käferfeuer
der Malven. Ehe der Winter
kam, umflog uns der Fremde Schnee.

Holzhaus, der Wälder
Leben und schöne Vergängnis,
aufgehoben mit Flügeln,
her durch den Wind
wie über Meere gekommen
bist du, nun wohnen in deinem
Rauch die Kinder, hören
auf dein Getön.

Deine Stille, der Lauchduft
und der Nesseln bittere
Schärfe, die Brunnenkühle—
Freund, wir lebten einst
über dem Fluß, auf der Wälder
Schattenrand, mit verschränkten
Händen laß uns singen, singen
wieder vom alten Haus.

Wirf wie die Mädchen
einen Kranz über die Schulter fort,
weghin ruf; es müßte der Abendwind
fallen in die Birken,
müßte der Nebel gehn

The Log Cabin Above the River Vilia

Riverwood,
dark with owl hoot, moss-white
with cricket call, we once saw
this cabin upon the shore, gray
in the mallow's beetle-fire.
Before winter arrived,
we stood in swirls of foreign snow.

Log cabin, life
of the forest, passing thing
of beauty, borne up into the wind
by wings, as if come from the sea,
now the children dwell
amid your smoke,
listening for the sounds
you relay.

Your stillness, and the scent
of leek and bitter prick
of nettles, the cool of the well—
Friend, we once lived
overlooking the river, at the edge
of the forest shade, hands clasped,
let us sing of this old cabin,
again and again.

Throw a wreath over your shoulders
as those girls once did,
and shout out: let the evening wind
fall among the birches,
let the fog go lightly

leicht am Ufer, die Feuchte
ziehen ums Haus—,
wenn wir singen die alte
Zeit mit verschränkten Händen,
von den Freundinnen laut,
leiser vom Wald
und den Tieren draußen,
den Pferden am Wiesenberg.

Dunkel war's, wir kamen
unter den Birken. Nachts
gingen die Schmuggler vorüber
dumpfen Tritts. Um Neumond
einmal
stand der Fremde im Hof.
"Wie lebst du?" fragt' er. Alinka
saß im Fenster. Sie schrie:
"Türriegellos!"

upon the shore, let its damp
embrace this home—
when we sing of times gone by,
hands clasped,
when we sing out loud
of all our young loves, yet more softly
of the woods or the horses
upon the grassy slopes.

It had turned dark, we made our way
among the birches. At night
the smugglers passed by
with muffled steps. At one point
under the new moon
a stranger stood in the farmyard.
"You live here alone?" he asked.
From her window perch, Alinka yelled down:
"With unbolted doors!"

(August 13, 1957)

Wilna

Wilna, du reifer Holunder!
Mit grünen Augen
ist deine Wolfzeit versunken.
Ur und Bär und der Eber,
da sie erschreckte der Hornschrei
Giedimins, sie hielten
erst am Njemen atmend,
im Eichwald über dem Ufer,
äugten hinab. Es hat
Mickiewicz besungen der wilder
leuchtenden Tage Glanz
und das Düster. Doch leicht
einherflog die zärtliche Wilia.

Ach, der Himmel, ein weißes,
wehendes Tuch, geschwungen
schön von den Liedern der Dörfer.
Die Birkentänze
hell in die Felder davon—

Doch es singt Lizdejko
nicht mehr, der Bärtige schläft,
heißt es, im endlos zerspülten
Ufersand, wo aus dem See
Trakai sich hob, die dunkele
Burg, aus Schimmer der Vorwelt.

Seine Gesänge, den schweren
Ufern gleich, waldigen, alten,
die der Wilia entgegen
wandern, ihrem hüpfenden

Vilna

Vilna, ripe elder!
Your green-eyed
wolf-times lie submerged.
Aurochs and bear and boar,
frightened by the blasts
of Gediminas's horn, once caught
their breath on these Nieman shores,
gazing down upon its waters
from the oak woods.
Mickiewicz sang of the wild
light of those days
and of their gloom. But the gentle Vilia
just flowed on.

Ah the sky, a white cloth
aflutter in the breeze
of village song. The bright
dance of birches
in the distant fields—

Though Lizdeika sings
no more, the bearded one sleeps,
they say, in the endlessly eroding
sands of the shore, from whose lake
the dark fortress of Trakai arose
from the shimmer of bygone days.

His songs are like those weighty
wooded, age-old riverbanks
that sidle up
to the skipping waters

Gang, und den Winden von Wilna;
rauchigen, die um das Haupt
der herrlichen Tochter gegangen.

Stadt der Könige, immer
singen die Ebenen alle,
alle die weißen, vom Blut
bitter der Söhne,
dir mit des Weißbarts hallender
Stimme, wie Eisgang, mit schmerzlichem
Festgetön deiner Juden,
rotem Sausen der Kiefern zu.

of the Vilia while the misty winds
from Vilna settle a crown
upon her splendid daughter.

City of kings, all the plains
sing out to you forever,
all the white ones, bitter
with the blood of their sons, they sing to you
with the echo of ancestral voices,
like drift ice, they sing with the ache
of your Jews at their celebrations
or the red sighs of your pines.

(October 8, 1955)

Am Strom

Du kamst
den Mondweg, von Ostra Brama
kamst du herab, von des alten
Bildes Glanz. In die Schürze
bargst du die Arme. Den Weg
kamst du zum Strom.

Abendgeleucht, vergängliche
Mühsal aus Staub,
unter dem Windfall immer
und entschwunden im Schwalbenflug.

Mädchen,
dein Blick aus dem Röhricht.
Ich rief dich den langen Tag.
Füll mir die Hände mit Sand,
die Feuchte will ich, die Schwere.
Nun atmen wir tiefer die Finsternis.

Lauscht' ich über den Strom?
Dem Vogel nach oder drunten
dem Grundfisch?—"Lieber, immer
Sprunglaut hör ich und droben
Flügelschlag. Geh mir nicht fort."

By the River

You came
by the moon route, from Ostra Bama
down you came from the icon's
ancient gleam. You buried
your arms in her lap. Your path
took you to the river.

Evening lights, all your passing
troubles now gone to dust,
blown in the wind,
gone in a swallow's flight.

Girl,
peering from the reeds,
I called out to you the whole day long.
Fill my hands with sand,
the moist, the heavy kind.
Now we breathe the dark more deeply.

Did I catch any sound of bird
over the river, or of groundfish down below?
"Darling, I'm always hearing
the plash of fish or wingbeat
overhead. Don't leave me."

(June 19, 1958)

Der litauische Brunnen

Meine Wege aus Sand, der Himmel
über dem Weidengebüsch.
Brunnenholz, fahr hinauf.
Tränk mich mit Erde.

Stundenweit, Lerche, dein Lied,
dem Habicht zu Häupten.
Wenn dich der Säer hört,
der Schnitter hat dein vergessen.

Blickt ins gestürzte Feld,
die Wagen kommen, der Windschrei.
Schöpferin, lehn dich ins Licht.
Sing dir den Mund blaß.

The Lithuanian Well

My paths of sand, the sky
above the willow bushes.
Well-pole, arise!
Quench me with earth.

Lark, your song overflies
the hours of the hawk.
When the sower has heard you,
the reaper has forgotten.

Look at this buckled field,
the carts come, the wind shrieks.
Lean into the light, O goddess,
sing your mouth off.

(July 3, 1957)

Friedhof

Spieße und Stangen,
gegen den Himmel, Moosfahnen,
ein Wäldchen,
das den Hügel herabkommt.
Ein Heerzug. Alt.
Die Münder voll Gras.

Die gesungen voreinst.
Nun tönen, umrauscht,
Hörner, geborsten,
Rassellaut, Schnarren. Nun geh,
einer Stimme zu lauschen
überm Wasser, her durch den Ruderschlag
einem einfachen Ruf,

den vom Gehölz
der Verborgne,
der Winter, zurückschreit.

Graveyard

Spears and stakes
against the sky, banners of moss,
a small stand of trees
down the hill slope.
An army column. Of old.
Mouths stuffed with grass.

Those who were once praised in song
now echo forth again, visited
by the snarl and sputter
of broken trumpets. Go now
and attend to the voice
borne upon the waters by oar stroke,
a simple cry,

calling back,
now buried,
from the winter woods.

(November 25, 1959)

Gestorbene Sprache

Der mit den Flügeln schlägt
draußen, der an die Tür streift,
das ist dein Bruder, du hörst ihn.
Laurio sagt er, Wasser,
ein Bogen, farbenlos, tief.

Der kam herab mit dem Fluß,
um Muschel und Schnecke
treibend, ein Fächergewächs,
im Sand und war grün.

Warne sagt er und *wittan,*
die Krähe hat keinen Baum,
ich habe Macht, dich zu küssen,
ich wohne in deinem Ohr.

Sag ihm, du willst
ihn nicht hören—
er kommt, ein Otter, er kommt
hornissenschwärmig, er schreit,
eine Grille, er wächst mit dem Moor
unter dein Haus, in den Quellen
flüstert er, *smordis* vernimmst du,
dein Faulbaum wird welken,
morgen stirbt er am Zaun.

Dead Language

He whose wings beat
about the house and brush
against the door, this is your brother,
you hear him say *laurio*, water,
rainbow, deep, without color.

He came by way of the river,
adrift among the mussels
and snails, fanned out
among the sands, green.

Warne he says and *wittan*,
the crow is without a tree,
I have the power to kiss you,
I inhabit your ear.

Tell him you'd rather not
listen—
he comes, an otter, comes,
a hornet swarm, his cries
a cricket's, spreading like the bog
beneath your house, whispering
in the well, *smordis* is what you hear,
tomorrow by the fence your black alder
shall wither and die.

(April 17, 1960)

Dorfnacht

Finsternis, wenn der letzte
das Tor schließt und lehnt an den Himmel,
an den steinernen Fries,
Pferde mit aufgeworfnen
Häuptern, schnaubend, mit Mähnen,
Schatten darüber, steil,
Glanz, kaltes Feuer, wirbelnd,
hinunter, mondlos die Zeit.

Schlaf für den Letzten. Ruten
streichen die Hauswand. Wind,
komm, unvernehmbare Rede,
tief in der Kehle, Gewölk,
wie die Katze ihr Junges
rief, das Dunkel tiefer
lockte ins Haus.

Einer steht vor dem Fenster,
der andre mit rundem Hut
taucht in die Wälder, lauscht
einem Hundegebell, der Ferne,
die er nicht sehen wird, Wälder,
Ströme, die Ufer bereift.

Vogelkäfig, bittere
Harfe, ertönend, Schwingen
schlagen die Gitter an, Nacht,
sammle, schlürf ein auch die Tropfen
Salz und die Tropfen
Licht.

Village Night

Darkness, when the last soul
shuts the gate and leans against the sky,
against the stone frieze,
horses, their heads
held high, snorting, shadows
steep on their manes,
sheen, cold fire, swirling
downward, in moonless season.

Sleep for the last soul. Birch branches
brush the house wall. Wind,
come, inaudible speech
deep within your throat, clouds,
with the cat mewing
to her kittens, the house
lured deeper into the dark.

One stands by the window,
the other in his round hat
takes to the woods, alert
to the invisible barking of dogs
in the distance, forests, streams,
hoarfrost on the shores.

Birdcage, bitter
strains of the harp, flutter
of wings against fences. Night,
go gather up the drops of salt,
the drops of light,
and slurp them down.

(March 31, 1960)

Die Spur im Sand

Der blasse Alte
im verschossenen Kaftan.
Die Schläfenlocke wie voreinst. Aaron,
da kannte ich dein Haus.
Du trägst die Asche
im Schuh davon.

Der Bruder trieb
dich von der Tür. Ich ging
dir nach. Wie wehte um den Fuß
der Rock! Es blieb mir eine Spur
im Sand.

Dann sah ich
manchmal abends
von der Schneise
dich kommen, flüsternd.
Mit den weißen Händen
warfst du die Schneesaat
übers Scheunendach.

Weil deiner Väter Gott
uns noch die Jahre
wird heller färben, Aaron,
liegt die Spur
im Staub der Straßen,
find ich dich.
Und gehe.

The Trace in the Sand

The pale old man
in his tattered caftan.
The sidelocks, as in former times. Aaron,
I used to know your house.
You bear its ashes away
in your shoes.

My brother drove you
from the door. I followed
after you. How your cloak
flapped about your foot. I was left with a trace
in the sand.

There were times
I saw you make your evening
way down the lane
in a whisper.
With your white hands
you tossed the seeds of snow
over the barn roof.

Because the god of your fathers
promises to ever brighten
the colors of our years, Aaron,
the trace of this
lies in the street dust,
I shall find you.
And go.

Und deine Ferne
trag ich, dein Erwarten
auf meiner Schulter.

All your distance, all your expectation
here borne
upon my shoulders.

(August 12, 1954)

Litauische Lieder

Nachts, tieräugig, ein Strauch
bin ich, ein Baum am Tag,
ein Wasser im Mittagsschatten,
unter der Sonne das Gras.

Oder um den Abend
eine Kirche am Berg, wo der Liebste
aus und ein geht, ein weißer
Priester, und Lieder singt.

Durch die Welt
lieb ich ihn, der Mondstrahl
muß ich sein um die Tür,
um das Haus im Fichtendunkel.

Einst flieg ich auf
mit der Laubvögel Sprüche im späten
Jahr, wenn ihr Herz,
ein Hagelkorn, weiß ist.

Lithuanian Songs

By night, animal-eyed, I'm
a shrub, by day a tree, and
in the midday shade, I'm
water, grass beneath the sun.

Or evenings, a chapel on a hill
which my beloved, a white
priest, singer of songs,
enters and leaves.

Through the world I bear
my love for him, let me be
the moonbeams round his door,
the dark pines round his home.

Late in the year, let me dart up
like the leaf warbler,
when her hailstone
heart is white.

(July 18, 1957)

Die Sarmatische Ebene

Seele,
voll Dunkel, spät—
der Tag mit geöffneten
Pulsen, Bläue—
die Ebene singt.

Wer,
ihr wogendes Lied,
spricht es nach, an die Küste
gebannt, ihr Lied:
Meer, nach den Stürmen,
ihr Lied——

Aber
sie hören dich ja,
lauschen hinaus, die Städte,
weiß und von altem Getön
leise, an Ufern. Deine
Lüfte, ein schwerer Geruch,
wie Sand
auf sie zu.

Und
die Dörfer sind dein.
Dir am Grunde grünend,
mit Wegen,
schmal, zerstoßenes Glas
aus Tränen, an die Brandstatt
gelegt deiner Sommer:
die Aschenspur,

The Sarmatian Plain

Soul,
full of darkness, late—
against the open-
pulsed, sky-blue day—
sings the plain.

Who
repeats its song's sway
under the spell
of the coast?
The sea, after storms,
repeats it.

But
amid the bleached hush
of ancient rumor,
the towns listening in
on the shore also hear you.
Your breezes arrive
with a heavy smell
of sand.

And
the villages are yours
tracing a green path to you
along the crushed glass
of trails of tears,
across the scorched earth
of your summers:
the path of ashes

da das Vieh geht
weich, vor dem Dunkel,
atmend. Und ein Kind
folgt ihm
pfeifend, es ruft
von den Zäunen
die Greisin ihm nach.

——

Ebene,
riesiger Schlaf,
riesig von Träumen, dein Himmel
weit, ein Glockentor,
in der Wölbung die Lerchen,
hoch—

Ströme an deinen Hüften
hin, die feuchten
Schatten der Wälder, unzählig
das helle Gefild,

da die Völker geschritten
auf Straßen der Vögel
im frühen
Jahr ihre endlose Zeit,

die du bewahrst
aus Dunkel. Ich seh dich:
die schwere Schönheit
des ungesichtigen Tonhaupts
—Ischtar oder anderen Namens—,
gefunden im Schlamm.

taken by cattle
softly breathing
before dark. And a child
follows him
whistling, and the old woman
calls after him
from the fence.

—

Plain,
giant sleep,
big with dreams, the spread
of your sky, a bell tower,
the larks high up
in the eaves—

Rivers
stream round your flanks,
the damp forest shade, the bright
unending fields

traversed by all the peoples
following the bird routes
in the early year
of that endless time

you gathered for them
out of the dark. I see you:
the heavy beauty
of that eyeless clay head,
named Ishtar or somebody else,
discovered in the mud.

(May 27, 1956)

Gegenlicht

Dämmerung.
Wie das Grasland
hertreibt, die breite Strömung,
Ebenen. Kalt, unzeitig
der Mond. Ein Flügelschlag nun.

Auf den Ufern der Ströme,
weit,
als sie der weite
Himmel umarmt hielt,
hörten wir Singen
im Wälderschatten. Der Ahn
ging verwachsenen Gräben nach.

Vogelherz, leicht, befiederter
Stein auf dem Wind.
In die Nebel
fallend. Gras und die Erde
nehmen dich an, eine Spur
Tod, einen Schneckenpfad lang.

Aber
wer erträgt mich,
den Mann mit geschlossenen Augen,
bösen Mundes, mit Händen,
die halten nichts, der dem Strom
folgt, verdurstend,
der in den Regen
atmet die andere Zeit,
die nicht mehr kommt, die andre,
ungesagte, wie Wolken,

Counterlight

Dusk.
The spread of the grasslands,
the broad rivers,
plains. The moon, cold,
untimely. A wingbeat now.

On the riverbanks,
far off
in the sky's embrace,
we heard singing
in the forest shadows. The ancestor
made his way along
the overgrown ditches.

Bird heart, light, feathered
stone on wind.
Falling
into the mists. Earth and grass
take you on, a trace
of death, snail track's length.

But
who will put up with me,
a man with eyes closed
and angry mouth, his hands
holding nothing, who follows
the river, parched,
there in the rain,
breathing in that other time
now gone forever, that other
unspoken time, cloudlike,

ein Vogel mit offenen Schwingen,
zornig, gegen den Himmel,
ein Gegenlicht, wild.

birdlike, wings spread,
furious, against the sky,
that counterlight, wild.

(December 10, 1959)

2.
Pruzzische Elegie

Dir
ein Lied zu singen,
hell von zorniger Liebe—
dunkel aber, von Klage
bitter, wie Wiesenkräuter
naß, wie am Küstenhang die
kahlen Kiefern, ächzend
unter dem falben Frühwind,
brennend vor Abend—

deinen nie besungnen
Untergang, der uns ins Blut schlug
einst, als die Tage alle
vollhingen noch von erhellten
Kinderspielen, traumweiten—

damals in Wäldern der Heimat
über des grünen Meeres
schaumigem Anprall, wo uns
rauchender Opferhaine
Schauer befiel, vor Steinen,
bei lange eingesunknen
Gräberhügeln, verwachsnen
Burgwällen, unter der Linde,
nieder vor Alter, leicht—

wie hing Gerücht im Geäst ihr!
So in der Greisinnen Lieder
tönt noch,
kaum mehr zu deuten,
Anruf der Vorzeit—

2.

Pruzzian Elegy

Let me sing you
a song bright with the anger
of love, yet dark,
bitter with grief, dank
as meadow weed,
or those barren pines
upon the sea cliffs, creaking
in the bleak early wind,
aflame before evening—

a song, still unsung,
of your undoing, once
driven deep into our blood
when every day was still lit
by endless dreams of child's play

back then, in our homeland woods
beyond the green brunt
of the foaming sea, we
shuddered in the smoke
of sacrificial groves, among
the stones, by the sunken
burial mounds and ramparts
overgrown, beneath the lindens,
light, bent with age—

how the rumor of all of this hung
upon your branches!
How that faraway past
rang forth, unfathomable,
in the old women's songs,

wie vernahmen wir da
modernden, trüb verfärbten
Nachhalls Rest!
So von tiefen
Glocken bleibt, die zersprungen,
Schellengeklingel—

Volk
der schwarzen Wälder,
schwer andringender Flüsse,
kahler Haffe, des Meers!
Volk
der nächtigen Jagd,
der Herden und Sommergefilde!
Volk
Perkuns und Pikolls,
des ährenumkränzten Patrimpe!
Volk,
wie keines, der Freude!
wie keines, keines! des Todes—

Volk
der schwelenden Haine,
der brennenden Hütten, zerstampfter
Saaten, geröteter Ströme—
Volk,
geopfert dem sengenden
Blitzschlag; dein Schreien verhängt vom
Flammengewölke—
Volk,
vor des fremden Gottes
Mutter im röchelnden Springtanz
stürzend—
Wie vor ihrer erzenen

how we heard the wreckage
of its echo, dimmed, drained
of color. Of those deep
cracked bells
only a dull shiver
remains—

Folk
of the black forests,
of the surging rivers
and broad lagoons, seafolk!
Folk
of the night hunt,
of herds and summer fields!
Folk
of Perkūns and Peckols,
of Patrimpas, wreathed with wheat!
Folk
like no other, folk of joy,
like no other, folk of death—

Folk
of smoldering groves
and burning huts and trampled
seedlings and bloodstained streams—
Folk
sacrificed to the singe
of lightning, screams shrouded
in smoke and flame—
Folk
who danced your death rattle,
falling before the mother
of the alien god, O see how she strides
in the van of her brazen troops,

Heermacht sie schreitet, aufsteigend
über dem Wald! wie des Sohnes
Galgen ihr nachfolgt! ——

Namen reden von dir,
zertretenes Volk, Berghänge,
Flüsse, glanzlos noch oft,
Steine und Wege—
Lieder abends und Sagen,
das Rascheln der Eidechsen nennt dich
und, wie Wasser im Moor,
heut ein Gesang, vor Klage
arm—

arm wie des Fischers Netzzug,
jenes weißhaarigen, ew'gen
am Haff, wenn die Sonne
herabkommt.

O see how she soars
over the woods, ahead of the gibbet
of her Son!—

The names still speak of you,
Folk crushed underfoot,
the hillsides, the rivers, the chance
stones and lanes—
campfire songs and sagas,
the flick of a lizard names you
as does this song,
today, like marsh water, poor
with grieving—

poor as the catch of the fisherman,
who, white-haired,
at sunset, recasts his net
into the lagoon.

(July 1952)

3.
Villon

Du, die Landschaft Touraine
durchstreifend: Steingrund
großer Städte immer
unter den Schritten, du
kommst nicht zurück.

Mond
hinter dir, schräg,
die langen Schatten voraus
vom Getürm und den Bäumen.
Einer geht da, pfeifend.
Den umhängt mit flüchtigen
kleinen Wolken—Chitongeweb—
der Diebsgott, ein griechischer, heißt's.

Kahlkopf, schwenk den Hut!
Dein Bild auf den mördrischen Spiegeln
aller Weiher! Im windigen Nord
weit das Fischernest:
unter der Mauer, im schiefen
Dach, in den Nebeln,
wirst du schlafen, die Männer
kommen morgens vom Fang, das Getränk
steht an den Herd gerückt,
da springt in den Pfannen der lautlose
Martyr, er glänzt vom Öl,
der Meerfisch.—"Da werd ich schlafen."

3.
Villon

You, fleeing your way
across the landscapes of Touraine,
cobblestoned towns
forever underfoot: you
shall never return.

The sharp slant
of the moon behind you,
the long strides
along towers and trees.
Someone walking there, whistling.
Hovering above him amid the small
shifting clouds—a chiton weave—
the god of thieves, said to be Greek.

Baldy, doff your hat!
Your mug shot on the murderous mirror
of every pond. The fishing spot
far in the windswept north:
by the wall, under the skewed
roof, amid the mists,
you shall sleep, the men
returning mornings with their catch,
the drink at hearth's edge,
the silent martyr leaping
into the pan, glistening with oil,
the fish of the sea. —"There I'll lay me down to sleep."

(March 2, 1957)

Góngora

Schwerthieb
im ersten Licht, des Corduaners
Zeile löst dir die Herzhaut ab:
dünn, Papier, bemalt
mit fliegenden Schwänen.

Ach, dunkelen Rufs,
der Schwäne Zug. Eine Feder,
weiß,
fällt auf dich zu. Du sollst
einen Namen schreiben
an den Himmel aus Feuer
—Don Luis' Namen—
in das Schweigen des heißesten Tags.

Denn die Treppe hinab,
in einem Schwarm Jungen, kommt Lorca.
Ach, Andalusier, Kinder! Er singt: Iberien,
schwarze Stimme, verwittert,
alt von der Könige Tritt.
Freunde, kommt weiß!
Mädchen, Licht, labyrinthischer
Tanz, labyrinthischer Tanz,

Nacht
oder, schmal,
ein geschliffner Saphir,
Irrsinn stürz auf die Schläfe
—einst auf Don Luis' Schläfe—
mitten im Schlaf.

Góngora

Sword thrust
in the first light, the Cordovan's
verse peels the skin from your heart:
paper-thin, painted
with swans in flight.

Ah, the dark cry
of swans on the wing. A feather,
white,
drifts down on you. Upon the sky
you shall go write a name
composed of fire—
the name of Don Luis—
in the still of the hottest day.

For here, down the steps,
in a swarm of boys, comes Lorca.
Hola! all you Andalusian kids! He sings: Iberia,
black-voiced, weathered,
ravaged by the tread of kings.
Amigos, turn up in white!
Girls galore, light, and the dance
labyrinthine, labyrinthine,

Night,
or finely chiseled
sapphire,
madness, crash down upon the brow
as you once did to Don Luis
in the midst of sleep.

(June 14, 1959)

Joseph Conrad

Linien,
über der Kimmung,
leicht, falbes Gebirg. Der Streifen
Weiß. Dort geht
zu Ende die Flut. Der Küste
Fiebergrün scheint herauf.

Und der Wind
fährt, ein Sprung in der Wölbung
aus Licht, bleiernem Licht. Das Schiff
aber ist da. Hier steh ich. Ich hab in den Lungen
die unaufhörliche Ferne.
Und sag deinen Namen,
mein Schiff.

Einmal, im hellen Abend,
wie der Habicht der Berge um Tschernigow,
blick ich hinaus, weißblühende
Städtchen, am Dnjestr gesungen,
hör ich, ich rufe den polnischen
Zimmermann. Dort,
sag ich, die Boote sind schwarz.
Das hab ich vergessen.

Himmel über uns, Ferne
bis unter die Segel, dunkelnd.
Und, inmitten, die brennende
Treue der Männer, gekommen
über die Meerflut.

Joseph Conrad

Lines,
on the horizon,
faint dusky hills. A streak
of white. Here the floodtide
ceases. Here the coast
gleams fever-green.

And the wind
drives on, leaping in the arc
of light, the leaden light. But the ship
has finally made it. Here I stand, the endless
distance within my lungs.
And say your name,
my ship.

One fine evening,
like some hawk of the hills around Chernigov,
I'll look out to catch wind of the small hamlets,
their white blossoms so praised all along
the Dniester, and I'll call out
to the Polish carpenter. There,
I say, the boats are black.
I had forgotten that.

Sky above us. The distance
darkening into our sails.
And, amid this, the fierce
loyalty of the men, come this far
over the fearsome waves.

(July 3, 1956)

Dylan Thomas

Marlais, der Clown,
gespitzten Munds
schmeckt er die Luft. Vom Ohio
steigt sie herauf. Und Missouri
kommt. Seines alten Schweigens
gewaltiger Lärm.

Zeit, in den Wind gebaut,
Mauern aus Licht. Ariadne—
ihr Gesicht vor die Dämmrung geschrieben,
Zeichen, der Fledermäuse
Tanz,—Labyrinth.

Nur im Augenwinkel
das Nest,
grau, der Küste Gesträuch, unermüdlich
redende Stimme
Swansea,
ein ertrunkener Schiffer,
der den Nebelweg kommt.

Marlais,
dem Wimperstreif folg,
einem zornigen Schwalbenflügel,
ehe der Strom
rauscht, die Wasser heraufgehn
um die Mauer, Babel ertrinkt, die verwirrte
Rede, Geschrei, von der Zinne
das Flüstern zuletzt.

Dylan Thomas

Marlais the clown
with pursed lips
tastes the breeze that blows
from the Ohio, and then
the Missouri. The loud boom
of what he once kept mum.

Time when walls were built
of light in the wind. Ariadne,
her face traced across the dusk,
signs, the dance
of bats—labyrinth.

Yet at the eye's canthus,
the nest, gray,
of all this coastal scrub, this unflagging
gab
of Swansea,
a drowned sailor
lurching through the mist.

Marlais,
follow the swat of your eyelashes,
an angry swallow's wing,
before the river rises
and the waters overspill
the walls, before Babel drowns, the clueless
rants and screams, down from the ramparts,
in the end, the whisperings.

(May 1959)

4.
Der Singschwan

Lieder der Hirten
langhin
auf der Welle von Blut,
er erkennt euch:
der heraufkommt, der Singschwan,
gelbschnäblig
dem berstenden Eis
folgt. Wir hören ihn dunkel,
wir trafen die Hirten,
über den Mooren schliefen
die Birkenwinde. Leise
war unsre Rede,
ein Feuer,
gefallen zur Nacht.

Flüsse, eueres Sinnes
werden wir sein im wehenden
Jahr, auf dem Quellgrund des Sommers,
lauschend: der Singschwan entfliegt,
und es tönt von der Heerfahrt
Igors das traurige Lied,
gesungen auf Türmen
in weißer,
hauchender Luft.

4.
The Whooper Swan

O songs of shepherds
carried from afar
on the wave-crest of blood,
he recognizes you,
this singing swan, rising
yellow-beaked
from the debris
of shattered ice. We hear him
in the dark, and as the winds
in the beech trees crept over the marshes,
we met the shepherds.
We spoke softly,
campfire
subsiding into night.

Rivers, we shall be
attuned to you at the turn
of the year, listening in
for the first trickles of summer:
the whooper swan takes wing
as the sad Song of Igor's Campaign
echoes forth,
told upon the towers
in a white whiff of air.

(August 6, 1956)

Windmühle

Licht,
schäumendes Licht,
über der Ebene, steil,
Berg aus Glanz, ungeheures
Rauschen, es fliegen die Stürme,
atmend von Blitzen, die schreckliche Wand
steigt an den Himmel.

Über die Düne,
vom Meer,
im baumlosen Schwemmland
bin ich gegangen,
schattenlos, traumlos, ich ging
mit den Schnittern, es stand die Mühle
starr und alt. Nun mit grauen
Flügeln greift sie die Lüfte.
Lautlos hebt sie sich auf überm Land.

Mit den Reihern davon
fährt sie, groß vor den weißen
Himmeln. Wild aus der Ferne
glänzt ihr das Auge
des Winters nach.

Eisvogel Herz,
aus Gräten und Flossen
bau dein Nest in der Höhlung,
im flüsternden Blut.

Bei den Kindern der Ebene, Töchtern und Söhnen,
bleib, bei den kleinen Schatten

Windmill

Light,
light frothing
across the plain, steep
mountain glow, unbelievable
noise, the storms on high
gulping up the lightning, a wall
of terror rising against the sky.

Over the seaward
dunes, across the barren swamps
I made my way
without dream or shade, walking
with the harvesters, the mill
looming over them, stiff and old. Now
on its gray wings it takes
to the air, soundlessly lifting
over the plain.

With the herons it flies away,
immense against the white
of the sky. Wild
in the distance, pursued by
winter's bright eye.

Ice-bird heart,
craft your nest
of fin and fishbone
from this hollow murmur of blood.

Cleave to the children of the plain,
amid the tiny shadows of their song

aus Liedern und Tänzen, du
halt ein Novembergras
gegen den Schnee.

and dance, hold a sprig
of November grass
against the snow.

(August 6, 1959)

Dorfstraße

Arglos der Sommer:
er geht mit den Flüssen—
listig und heiß:
die Rosen brechen herauf.
Bald die Fröste Skythiens,
flammend und innen
ein Rauchgestein, schwarz.

Dorther,
von den randlosen
Himmeln kommt er,
hinter der Stute, der Pflüger,
in der Rjasanschen Birke,
hoch im Gezweig,
stehn die Gewitter, erbeben
sieht er das Ufer, die weite
Ebene schwankt.

Mikula, wunderbarer
Pflüger im hölzernen Rußland,
heiteren Mundes komm
an die Tränke, wir werden singen,
Strophen singen aus nichts als Wind.
Einmal abends die Stimme
tönt, Tschaadajews Stimme,
atmend in der Verzweiflung,
ein Vogelschrei.

Wege:
Räderspur,
Hufspur,

Village Road

O carefree summer,
running with the rivers,
sweltering, wily,
all the roses out in bloom.
Soon followed by the Scythian
frosts, fireplace flames, soot
on stone hearth, black.

There,
from the outer reaches
of the sky, here he comes
behind his mare, the plowman,
thunderstorms gathered
high in boughs
of the Ryazan birches,
he sees the shore begin to tremble
and the broad plain sway.

Mikula, O wondrous plowman
of these Russian woods,
step up and take a glad
gulp of drink. Let's sing strophes
made of nothing but wind.
One evening even the voice of
Chaadayev might be heard,
a bird catching its breath
from despair.

Routes:
wheel tracks,
hoof prints,

Kraut
und der Staub—
der Erde Gesicht,
auf den Grund der Flüsse gelegt,
in den Sand,
den die Strömung treibt.
Und in mein Herz. Nie mehr
tauchts nun herauf.

weeds
and dust—
the face of the earth
laid upon the riverbeds
and upon the shifting sands.
And upon my heart. Which shall now
surface no more.

(July 3, 1959)

Die Kirche
"Lindere meinen Kummer"

Über den Wänden,
Stein, über den Bögen
die Kuppeln aus Wind, gefügt
unter den Himmel, alt,
der mit Fähren und Flößen kommt,
der vor den Abenden her
singt, Bienenrauch fährt mit ihm, Atem
vom Himbeerstrauch, spät—

wenn die Herrin der Felder,
runden Auges, weißhaarig,
erstarrt mit den schmalen Armen,
leicht, eine Esche,
Hände aus Laub wie Gewölk,
der Moore bittere Luft
fängt und den Trunk
führt an den Mund.

The Church "Assuage My Sorrows"

Over the walls,
stone, over the arches
and cupolas of wind, age-old
stone raised heavenward,
imported here by raft and ferry,
singing out before dusk,
freighted with bee smoke and breath
of raspberry bush, late—

when Our Lady of the Fields,
round of eye, white of hair,
frail of arm, light
as ash bough, reaches out
her leafy cloudlike hands
to cup the bitter marsh air
and raise the potion
to her lips.

(April 5, 1960)

Auf der Taurischen Straße

Dieser Abend: im Wind—
Wasser, es trägt uns fort
über der Tiefe—
oder die halbe Nacht
kommt auf der Wachtel ängstlichem
Fluchtweg, mit bebenden Flügeln—

Einmal
am Rand der Steppe,
wir kamen vom Gurkenfeld,
an der Straße lagerten
die Kamele. Eines
hob sich auf, weitäugig
aus alter Schönheit, sah nach der großen Tiere
Ferne, im Dunst der Kaspischen See.
Dahinter Enkidu:

wie er nahte
von der Gazellen Tränke,
finstren Gesichts. Ich bin auf der Steppe geboren,
sagt er, kämpfen werd ich
im Zedernwald.

On the Tauric Road

This evening: in the wind,
the water bears us onward
over the deeps,
or the half night
arrives on the quail's fearful
flutters of flight—

Once
at the edge of the steppe,
we came across a field of cucumbers,
camels resting by the road. One of which
arose, wide-eyed
in its ageless beauty, gazing upon
the great beasts in the distance
across the mists of the Caspian Sea.
With Enkidu behind all this:

he approached
the gazelle's waterholes,
his face glowering: I was born on the steppes,
said he, and in this cedar wood
shall make my stand.

(October 16, 1958)

Landschaft mit Vögeln

Alt, vorjähriges Gras
die Ebene, größer, die Hügel
alle versunken. Der See
weiß, verdehnt an den Horizont.
Dorther der Kranich. Hoch.
Über dem Licht. Dem eigenen
Schatten nach.

Und eine Stimme
wie ein Gehölz und voll grüner
Schatten, feucht, wenn das Wasser
zurückgeht. Lerche, der Stein
barst, auf dem du gesungen
Morgen um Morgen
vorm Lederzelt. Nur der Eine
hat dich gehört, erwachend,
Temudschin
hat dich gehört.

Einst, die ewige Zeit
geschlafen, vermauert, die Höhle
brachen sie auf, sieben Männer,
traten hervor. Ein Baum
hat mich umwachsen, mit harten
Rinden, wie Schlaf, im Gezweig
droben der Rabe
strählt sein Gefieder. Mein Baum,
zitternd, wo dich mein Herz
anschlägt, winterlich, aber
reißen wird deine Rinde nicht.

Landscape with Birds

Old, last year's
grass on the plains, vaster
with the hills slung low. The lake,
white, spread out on the horizon.
The crane there. High.
Above the light. Pursuing
its own shadow.

And a voice
like a grove, full of green
shade, damp, when the water
recedes. O lark, the stone
is shattered, upon which
every morning
by the leather tent
you used to sing. Only one soul
heard you upon waking,
Temujin heard you.

Back then, having slept,
walled-up, for an eternity,
they broke open the cave,
and seven men strode forth.
A tree has grown up about me,
its bark as tough as sleep, up there
in its branches the raven
preens. My tree trembles
where my wintry heart
beats against you, but
your bark will not split its seams.

Ob auch der Schnee
herabstäubt
einst,
wenn der Rabe den Flügel rührt.

Even if the snow
powders down
when the raven
shrugs its wing.

(January 7, 1960)

Steppe

Einer war,
der sang in den Abend. Draußen
schwer die Ebene,
baumlos, um niedres Gewächs
brennend der Sand—
da hielten die Wolken dunkel,
und ein Mond hing herab.
An dem Wasserloch falb
die Herde. Einer, braunbärtig,
kam, er trieb die Rinder
fort. Im Fenster der andere sang.

Dörfer,
wie will ich leben
noch? In der Ferne weiß ich
endlos rinnender Himmel
Glanz. Den Jungen, der sang,
und den Hüter mit hellen
Augen hörte ich reden
an der Straße, ich stand,
im Rücken das Dorf.

Steppe

There was one
who sang in the evening. Outside,
the heavy plain,
treeless, the scorch
of sand on scrub,
cloud and moon
slung there in the dark.
At the waterhole, the dusky
herd. Someone, brown-bearded,
came and drove the cattle
off. The other sang at the window.

Villages,
how shall I go on
living? In the distance I know
the endless sheen of rippled rain. The boy,
singing, and the herdsman with the bright
eyes, I heard them talking
by the wayside,
as I stood there,
village at my back.

(April 11, 1956)

Der Ilmensee 1941

Wildnis. Gegen den Wind.
Erstarrt. In den Sand
eingesunken der Fluß.
Verkohltes Gezweig:
das Dorf vor der Lichtung. Damals
sahn wir den See—

—Tage den See. Aus Licht.
In der Wegspur, im Gras
draußen der Turm,
weiß, fort wie der Tote von seinem
Stein. Das geborstene Dach
im Krähengeschrei.
—Nächte den See. Der Wald.
In die Moore hinab
fällt er. Den alten Wolf,
fett von der Brandstatt,
schreckte ein Schattengesicht.
—Jahre den See. Die erzene
Flut. Der Gewässer steigende
Finsternis. Aus den Himmeln
einmal
schlägt sie den Vogelsturm.

Sahst du das Segel? Feuer
stand in der Weite. Der Wolf
trat auf die Lichtung.
Hört nach des Winters Schellen.
Heult nach der ungeheuren
Wolke aus Schnee.

Lake Ilmen 1941

Wilderness. Against the wind.
Numbed. The river
sunk into the sand.
Charred branches:
the village by the clearing. Back then
we beheld the lake—

—Lake days. Days of light.
Along the path, in the grass
beyond, the tower, white,
like a dead man gone
from his grave. The roof collapsed
amid the caw of crows.
—Lake nights. The forest
sinking into the marshes.
The old wolf, fattened up
on the ruins, startled
by the face of a ghost.
—Lake years. The iron
tide. The rising dark
of the waters. Which one day
shall strike the bird-
storm from the sky.

Did you see the sail? Fire
in the plain. The wolf
crossed the clearing.
He cocks an ear to the winter bells.
Howls at the huge
cloud of snow.

(June 1959)

Stromgedicht

Traum,
jählings,
aus Feuern der Habichtsnacht,
Tieraug,
Blitz unter reglosem Lid
vor, Pfeilbündel Schilf,
wo der Otter, ein Herzsprung,
taucht.

Vor den Aufschein,
die weiße
Mauer aus Licht,
vor den steigenden
Horizont, von Geschrei überglänzt,
von der Tiefe erhoben,
über die Finsternis,
dem ruhlosen Tierherz,
Fraß und Brut,

tritt der Strom,
er kommt
waffenlos, ein anderer
Held, der schlang seine Kindheit
ein, es ist der Wald nun
die Speise und folgt ihm

an den Berg,
an die Schwärze auf
—der Kalmus im Schwerttanz
glänzt vor dem Tag—,
in das Dunkel der Brüche

River Poem

Dream,
sudden, arisen
from hawk-night fires,
flash of animal eyes
from unblinking lids,
reeds, arrow quivers into which
the otter, in a heart leap,
dives.

Before the rising
of the white
wall of light,
before the climb
of the horizon, lit with cries,
risen from the depths
of the dark,
animal-heart, restless,
feeding, spawning,

the river steps up
unarmed, another
hero who wolfed
his childhood down
and now takes bites
of the forest, following it

uphill
into the gloom
(calamus sword dance
at the break of dawn),
into the dark of the fens,

bis an das Dunstland: Inseln,
schwebend, Morast, gestürzte
Tore, eingesunkene
Bögen, Fahnen aus Vogelgeripp
und Tang—
auf dem Schlick
stirbt er, auf den Watten
noch Spur seines Atems, Möwen
decken sie zu.

Traum,
mit des Habichts Schrei
endend, dem Rauschen,
hoch,
Zeichen an bläulicher Wand,
gekratzt in den Mörtel
mit dem Nagelrand, Bild,
Abbild,
sarmatisch,

lange
folg ich dir,
Strom,
an Rändern der Wälder,
ermattend
leicht, im alten
Zinn ein Geräusch.

into the haze of the plains: isles
afloat, swamps, broken
gates, sunken arches, flags
of seaweed and skeleton birds,
amid the slime
the river dies,
the trace of its breath
on the mudflats
trampled by the gulls.

Dream,
ending with a hawk
cry, with a roar
overhead, with
signs on the sky-
blue wall, scratched into
the mortar by a fingernail, image
afterimage,
Sarmatian,

river, long
have I followed you
at forests' edge,
easily
fatigued, your sound
dull
as ancient tin.

(May 11, 1959)

Die Heimat des Malers Chagall

Noch um die Häuser
der Wälder trockener Duft,
Rauschbeere und Erdmoos.
Und die Wolke Abend,
sinkend um Witebsk, aus eigener
Finsternis tönend. Ein schütt'res
Lachen darin, als der Ahn
lugte vom Dach
in den Hochzeitstag.

Und wir hingen in Träumen.
Aber es ist Verläßliches
um unsrer Väter Heimatgestirne gegangen,
bärtig, wie Engel, und zitternden Mundes,
mit Flügeln aus Weizenfeldern:

Nähe des Künftigen, dieser
brennende Hörnerschall,
da es dunkelt, die Stadt
schwimmt durch Gewölk,
rot.

The Painter Chagall's Homeland

Around the houses
the lingering dry forest scent
of huckleberry and club moss.
And the evening cloud
settling over Vitebsk, echoing forth
from its own dark. A quiet chuckle
amid all this, as grandpa
eyed the wedding feast
from the roof.

And we were lost in dreams.
Yet trusted in those stars that seeded
the homeland of our fathers,
bearded, like angels, mouths
aflutter with wheatfield wings:

The nearness of what's to come, this
burning blast of the shofar horn,
at nightfall, the town,
red,
swims through the clouds.

(July 1, 1955)

Lettische Lieder

Mein Vater der Habicht.
Großvater der Wolf.
Und der Ältervater der räubrische Fisch im Meer.

Ich, unbärtig, ein Narr,
an den Zäunen taumelnd,
mit schwarzen Händen
würgend ein Lamm um das Frühlicht. Ich,

der die Tiere schlug
statt des weißen
Herrn, ich folg auf zerspülten
Wegen dem Rasselzug,

durch der Zigeunerweiber
Blicke geh ich. Dann
am baltischen Ufer treff ich den Uexküll, den Herrn.
Er geht unterm Mond.

Ihm redet die Finsternis nach.

Latvian Songs

My father the hawk.
My grandfather the wolf.
And my forefather the rapacious fish in the sea.

I, beardless, a fool
crashing through fences,
with my black hands I throttled
a lamb in the early light. I,

who struck out at animals
instead of the white
lord, I follow the caravans
rattling down the washed-out roads,

making my way among the Gypsy women's
stares. Then on the Baltic shore
I come across Uexküll, the lord,
walking beneath the moon.

His words echoed by the dark.

(October 23, 1956)

Die Düna

Düna, Morgenfrühe
immer um dich und der herrliche
Wind der Ebnen. Die alte
Stadt liegt im Rauch.

Kalt deine Ufer. Buschwerk,
ein grüner Streif. Deine Schwalben
jagen hinauf
ins Licht.

Müd
um den Mittag
bin ich gekommen,
ich fall auf den Sand.
Ich will vom Atem der Ströme
leben, vom Sprind
trinken, das Irdische trinken,
die Nacht, vom Geheimnis der Tiefe
unter dem Gras.

Leben im Feuer des Tags
will ich, die Flammen teilen,
dich zu sehn: Im steigenden Jahr
schweren Mundes gehst du,
dunkel—die Möwen
sprühn und die Wasser auf,
schreiend empfängt dich das Meer—
du gehst ihm entgegen.

The Düna

Düna, never far
from the dawn or the splendid
wind of the plains. The ancient
town lies in smoke.

Your shores cold. Bushes,
a strip of green. Your swallows
hunt up
into the light.

Dead tired,
around noon, I arrived,
I fall upon the sand.
Let me live upon the breath
of rivers, let me drink
from their springs, let me
drink of the earth,
of the night, of the deep secrets
buried beneath the grass.

Let me live in the fire
of day and part its flames
to see you: toward year's end,
heavy of mouth, you make
your dark advance, the screaming sea
inviting you through the spray
of gull and wave to edge
in its direction.

In seinem Schatten,
vom Grund
das alte Getier
seufzt dir zu.

In its shadows,
from its deeps,
the ancient creatures
sigh out to you.

(March 24, 1959)

Nachtweg

Leicht,
zu belauern die Sterne,
alte Bilder: Stier und
Schwan und den Fährmann,—
wär ich ein Nachtgesträuch,
eine Ranke, schwarz vom Tau, um die Freundin
Dryas geschlungen—
leicht,
zu singen das Nebellied.

Aber der Mond, ein durchscheinendes
altes Metall—keiner mehr weiß es—
tönt den Vogelheeren
zu, dem rufenden Wanderkeil
droben. Oder vielleicht
nach den Tänzern der Mitternacht.

Über dem Talsturz einst
sah sie der Ahn:
schmal, mit spitzen Schritten. Im Feldwind, ich
hörte Geschrei wie von schnellen
Wagen herab, die Hunde
flogen vorbei, vor dem Reiter
her. Ich horchte
an der Weide
dem Jagdvolk nach.

Nightway

How easy
to lie in wait for the ancient
pictures of the stars: the Bull,
the Swan, the Charioteer—
were I a bush at night,
or a tendril black with dew, draped about the neck
of my sweet Dryad—
how easy
to sing the music of the mists.

But the moon, this old translucent
metal disk—unbeknownst
to all—rings out to the serried ranks
of birds, their battle cries wedged
overhead. Or perhaps
to the midnight dancers.

Over the valley's rim
the ancestor
once espied them:
slender, on pointe. In the field-wind
I heard screams
as from rushing chariots, the hounds
flying by, ahead of
the riders. I stood in the meadow,
listening for the hunters.

(April 30, 1958)

Kaunas 1941

Stadt,
über dem Strom ein Gezweig,
kupferfarben, wie Festgerät. Aus der Tiefe die Ufer
rufen. Das hüftkranke Mädchen
trat vor die Dämmerung damals,
sein Rock aus dunkelstem Rot.

Und ich erkenne die Stufen,
den Hang, dieses Haus. Da ist kein
Feuer. Unter dem Dach
lebt die Jüdin, lebt in der Juden Verstummen,
flüsternd, ein weißes Wasser
der Töchter Gesicht. Am Tor
lärmen die Mörder vorüber. Weich
gehn wir, im Moderduft, in der Wölfe Spur.

Abends sahn wir hinaus
auf ein steinernes Tal. Der Habicht schwebte
um die breite Kuppel.
Sahen die Stadt, alt, Häusergewirr hinunter
bis an den Strom.

Wirst du über den Hügel
gehn? Die grauen Züge
—Greise und manchmal die Knaben—
sterben dort. Sie gehn
über den Hang, vor den jachernden Wölfen her.

Sah ich dich nicht mehr an,
Bruder? An blutiger Wand
schlug uns Schlaf. So sind wir

Kaunas 1941

Town,
copper-colored candelabra
branch upon the river. The shores
call out from the deep. The girl
with the lame hip limped through the dusk,
her skirt the darkest red.

And I recognize the stairs,
the hillside, this house. No fire
here. Under this roof
lives the Jewess, whispering
in the Jewish hush, her daughters' faces
white as water. The murderers
holler at the gate. We slink
through the musty air, in the tracks of wolves.

Evenings we looked out
upon a valley of stones. The hawk swept
round the broad dome.
We saw the town, its maze of houses
reaching the river.

Will you cross over
the hill? There the gray columns
of old men and stray boys
go to their death, moving up
the slope, ahead of the slavering wolves.

Did my eyes avoid yours,
brother? By the bloodstained wall
we were struck by sleep. Then proceeded

weitergegangen, um alles
blind. Im Eichwald draußen
mit der Zigeuner Blick die Dörfer, hinauf um die Firste
des Sommers Schnee.

Tief im Regengesträuch
werd ich treten den Uferstein,
lauschen im Dunst der Ebenen. Da waren die Schwalben
stromhinauf und die Nacht
grün, die Waldtaube rief:
Mein Dunkel ist schon gekommen.

onward, blind to everything.
Out in the oak woods, the villages
with their Gypsy stares, summer snow
upon their roofs

I shall walk the stone banks
through the rain-soaked bushes, listening in
to the mist of the plains. Swallows
upstream and the night green,
the wood pigeon calling:
My dark is already come.

(June 1958)

Wiederkehr

Holzbank, ein hartes meuble.
Dort, zwischen Kiefernbäumen,
die Schaukel—ein Brett, zwei geschälte
Stangen. Vorbei kommt der Kuckuck,
Blaurake und Wiedehopf,
Nachtigall, die ein Sprosser ist,
kürzer singt, lakonischer,
rauher, gebs Gott.

Aber ich kam zu schlafen
unter der Balkenwand,
Schlaf aus Spinnweb und Krötengold,
fliegenbeinigen Schlaf. Zurück
geht das Licht. Um ihre Schatten herum
tappen die Kühe. Der Fisch
reißt ein schäumendes Zeichen
über das Wasser.

Aber ich schlaf nur.
Ich bin nicht hier.
Ich such eine Stelle,
nur ein Grab breit, den kleinen Berg
über den Wiesen. Von dort
kann ich sehen
den Fluß.

Return

Bench, a solid *meuble*.
There, between the pines, the swing—
a board, two ingenious poles. Flying by,
the cuckoo, the blue roller, the hoopoe,
then the nightingale, a sprosser
quicker, more
laconic, hoarser
in song, God willing.

But I came here to sleep
by the log wall,
gossamer, toad-gold,
fly-legged sleep. The light
recedes. The cows stumble
over their shadows. The fish
strikes a stripe of foam
across the waters.

But all I do is sleep.
I'm not here.
I seek a place
no wider than a grave, a small hill
above the meadows. From which
to catch sight
of the river.

(February 22, 1960)

Feuer und Schnee

Feuer,
das Birkengehölz
brennt, aus der schwärzlichen Woge,
aus dem Gewölk
Qualm
schlägt die Flamme,
der wilde Tanz Flammen, Verlockung
fährt auf die Haut, Verlockung
Flamme—

Im Meer
ist eine Straße, ein großes
Tieraug, weinend und weit
offen, die grüne Wimper
über der Wange aus Salz,
Kühle, Verlockung
Kühle—

Beides
der junge Mensch,
Verlockung Flamme, Verlockung
Kühle, der Tanz
über der Wolke, die Kühle
Salz oder Schnee, der junge
Mensch in der ersten
Tagstunde, schön von Erschöpfung,
das Haupt aus Schatten
gefügt.

In meinem Atem,
Feuer und Schnee, ich lebe.

Fire and Snow

Fire,
the birchwood
burning, from the black waves,
from the billows of smoke,
the flames shoot out,
dancing wildly,
seducing
the skin with the lure
of flame—

In the sea
lies a road, a great
animal eye, weeping,
its green eyelids open wide
above its salty cheeks,
cold, the lure
cold—

Both these,
for the young man,
the lure of flame, the lure
of cold, the dance
over cloud, the cold
of salt or snow, the young
man in the first hour
of day, how lovely
his exhaustion, his head
shaped by shadows.

In my breath,
fire and snow,

So kommst du im Feuer,
so kommst du
morgen im Schnee.

I make my home.
Here you come as fire.
Tomorrow you'll come as snow.

(October 29, 1959)

Seeufer

Was noch lebt
im Treibsand
unter der großen Fische
Flossenflügel, schwindendes
Grün, Algen, ein Seemoos,
das den Mond bewächst,
morgens, wenn er ertrinkt,

ist wie ein Wort, ungesagt,
gehört in der Höhlung des Mundes,
im Beben der Schläfe,
im Haar. Wir treiben ans Ufer,
mit bläulichen Händen Liebe,
weiß.

Komm,
es ist kalt, hören
wird uns das Stroh, die Decke
über dem Seufzer, die knisternde
Holzwand. Der Schlaf, ein Geflüster,
legt sich zu uns.

Lake Shore

What's still alive
in the quicksand
beneath the fins
of the big fish—dwindling
green, algae, whiteweed
clinging to the moon,
mornings, when it drowns,

is like a word, unspoken,
heard in the hollow of the mouth,
in the pulse of the temples,
in the hair. We drift shoreward,
hands blue, my love,
white.

Come,
it's cold out, the straw
shall hear us, the blanket
covering our sighs, the creak
of the wooden wall. A whisper of sleep
lies down by our side.

(March 23, 1960)

Einmal haben

Einmal haben
wir beide Hände voll Licht—
die Strophen der Nacht, die bewegten
Wasser treffen den Uferrand
wieder, den rauhen, augenlosen
Schlaf der Tiere im Schilf
nach der Umarmung—dann
stehen wir gegen den Hang
draußen, gegen den weißen
Himmel, der kalt
über den Berg
kommt, die Kaskade Glanz,
und erstarrt ist, Eis,
wie von Sternen herab.

Auf deiner Schläfe
will ich die kleine Zeit
leben, vergeßlich, lautlos
wandern lassen
mein Blut durch dein Herz.

One Day

One day
we'll have both hands full of light—
strophes of night, waters
again lapping the shores, meeting
with the ragged, eyeless sleep
of lovers in the reeds
after their embrace—and then
find ourselves on a hillside,
standing against the white
sky coming cold
over the heights,
cascade of light,
frozen ice, down
from the stars.

Let me linger awhile
upon your brow
and forget it all. Let my blood
wander through your heart
without a sound.

(February 18, 1960)

Die Memel

Hinter den Feldern, weit,
hinter den Wiesen
der Strom.
Von seinem Atem
aufweht die Nacht.
Über den Berg
fährt der Vogel und schreit.

Einmal mit dem Wind
gingen wir, stellten das Netz
in der Mündung des Wiesenbachs.
In den Erlen
hing die Laterne. Der Alte
nahm sie herab.
Das Schmugglerboot stieß auf den Sand.

Aus der Finsternis
kommst du, mein Strom,
aus den Wolken.
Wege fallen dir zu
und die Flüsse, Jura und Mitwa,
jung, aus Wäldern, und lehmschwer
Szeszupe. Mit Stangen die Flößer
treiben vorbei. Die Fähre
liegt auf dem Sand.

Und der Himmel
dunkelt von Vogelheeren.
In der Luft aus schlagenden Flügeln, hoch,
Schilflaut, Brunnenrauch, harziger Wälder Rauch.
An den Birken, über dem Ufer nun

The Memel

Far beyond the fields
and meadows,
the river.
The night rises
from its breath.
The bird drifts over the hill
and calls.

We once went
with the wind to fix our nets
at the mouth of the meadowbrook.
A lantern hung
in the alders. The old man
took it down. On the sand
the smugglers' boat ran aground.

Out of the dark,
you come, my river,
out of the clouds.
All roads lead to you
and to the other rivers, the Jura and the Mitva,
fresh from the woods, and to the loamy
Szezupe. The loggers pole
downstream. The ferry
lies on the sand.

And the sky darkens
with all its troops of birds.
Up in the air, amid the wingbeat,
reed-rustle, well-smoke, smoke
of the resinous woods.

stehn die Frauen, mit Bändern,
gelben und roten—eine,
an den gewölbten Leib
zieht sie die Töchter, die jungen
Söhne baden im Strom.

Strom,
alleine immer
kann ich dich lieben
nur.
Bild aus Schweigen.
Tafeln dem Künft'gen: mein Schrei.
Der nie dich erhielt.

Nun im Dunkel
halt ich dich fest.

Among the birch trees, on the riverbank,
the women now gather, beribboned
in yellows and reds—one of them
draws her daughters to her swollen belly,
her young boys gone swimming.

River,
ever alone,
it's only you
I can love.
Image of stillness.
A memorial to the future: my cry.
That never reached you.
Now in the dark
I hold you fast.

(June 16, 1959)

Die Daubas

Droben schwang der Wind.
Wir lebten am Fluß in den Hütten.
Dunkelnd die Ufer hinauf,
tönte das Schilf.

Wir waren Kinder mit unsern
Herzen. Die sangen uns jahrhin.
Anders nicht als die Erde
kamen Fröste und Regen,
Blitz und Gewölk, wie die Zeit—

wie die Zeit,
die wir nahmen
und gaben sie aus den Händen,
rot von Früchten. Die Winter
flossen ins Licht.

Das ist vergangen.
Wir ließen die Dörfer dem Sande.
Kaum wie ein Flößerruf
zogen wir fort.

Folgend der Bitternis, legen
wir Holz zu den Feuern der Fremde,
wissen ein Lied noch: einst
blühte der Apfelbaum.

Wo denn
wollen wir bleiben?
Immer ist es die Erde,
der Grund, da wir liegen werden.

The Daubas

The wind wavered back and forth
overhead. We lived in huts
by the river. The clatter of reeds
darkened the slope of the shore.

We were children
at heart, singing year in
year out. In tune with the earth
came frosts and rains,
lightning and clouds, like the time—

like the time
we took
and offered up with our own hands,
red with fruit. The winters
flowed into the light.

All this now gone.
We left the villages to the sands.
With less than a logger's cry
we went our way.

Thus embittered,
we toss wood on foreign fires,
remembering this song: That hour,
that apple tree in flower.

Where then
should we reside?
The earth will always be
the ground on which we lie.

Die Kinder
finden das Dorf nicht.

Aber die Gärten, der Schilfstrich
am Strom—jenes Uferland Daubas—
gilbende Scheunen—
und das Gespann, das vom Wald kam—
der Habicht im leeren Blau—

noch verfärbts uns die Blicke.
So treten wir unter den Bogen
dieser Jahre. Und zählen
unsre Freuden der Erde zu.—

Fühlend das Blut in den Schläfen,
das Haar zu streichen den Töchtern,
abends sprichst du: Komm,
Liebste, du bleibst noch—so
sehn ich mich nicht.

The children won't find
the village.

But the gardens, the swathes of reeds
by the river, the shorelines of the Daubas,
the yellowing barns,
the horse and cart down from the woods,
the hawk up in the empty blue—

these still color the scene.
So we advance beneath the arc
of these years. And ascribe
our blessings to the earth.

Feeling the blood pulse in your temples
as you stroke your daughters' hair,
evenings, you say: Come,
my love, you're still here—no need for me
to yearn.

(December 7, 1954)

Winterlicht

In dieser Nacht
lausch ich nach euch, ferne Flüsse,
euerem ersten Eis,
lange. Jenen schmalen
Binsenton hör ich; das Dorf
schläft.

Kindheit, bräunlich, ein kaltes
Brunnengewässer, sandig—
Immer schwang der hölzerne
Eimer hinunter. Wer kam?
löste von rostender Kette ihn?
ach, wer trank?

Unsrer Hütten dunkel
redende Güte, ihr sanftes
Wort ist verschneit,
Muhmengewisper und Kinderruf—

Zeit aus Fliederfarben
einst, da im ziehenden Himmel
hingen Vögel, im schwindenden
Schein; der Himmel
blieb stehn,
hielt überm Scheunendach, voller
schwieg er die Schatten herein.

Winter wurde es immer.
Mit Taubenflügeln kam
tiefer die Bläue, ein hängendes

Winterlight

On this night
I listen at length for you,
distant rivers, for your early ice.
I hear the thin sound
of the rushes; the village
sleeps.

Childhood, sepia, the cold
well water, sandy,
the wooden bucket forever
on a downward swing. Who came
to release it from its rusty chain?
Who was it took a drink?

The dark kindly talk
within our huts, all its tender words
now snowed in,
old aunts' whispers, children's shouts—

that former lilac-tinted
time when the birds hung
in the shifting sky, the light
declining, the sky
holding still, paused
above the barn roof,
inviting the shadows in.

Winter was always on its way.
The blue deepening
with pigeon wings, roof's

Dach, erschimmernd leise
über der Welt.

Und der Jägerschrei fuhr
an den Hang auf, schweigendem
Schnee entgegen. O tiefe
Schwärze! dein Herz
voller Licht!

overhang, quiet shimmer cast
upon the world.

And the hunters' cries
echoed up the slopes, toward
the silent snows. O deep
dark! Your heart
so full of light!

(December 23, 1955)

Absage

Feuer,
aus Blut die Lockung:
der schöne Mensch. Und wie Schlaf
das Vergangene, Träume
an Flüssen hinab,
auf den Wassern,
segellos, in der Strömung.

Ebenen—die verlornen
Dörfer, der Wälder Rand.
Und ein dünner Rauch
in den Lüften,
steil.

Einst,
wulstigen Munds, Perkun
kam, eine Feder im Bart,
kam in der Hufspur des Elchs,
der Stotterer kam,
fuhr auf den Strömen, Finsternis
zog er, ein Fischernetz, nach.

Dort
war ich. In alter Zeit.
Neues hat nie begonnen. Ich bin ein Mann,
mit seinem Weibe ein Leib,
der seine Kinder aufzieht
für eine Zeit ohne Angst.

Refusal

Fire,
the lure of blood:
Man, in all his perfection. And like sleep,
the past—dreams
driven downriver
by the currents, across
the waters, without a sail.

Plains—the villages
gone, the forests' edge.
Spindles of smoke
steep
in the breeze.

Time was
thick-lipped Perkūns
came, feather in his beard,
came, in elk's track,
the stutterer came,
traveling the river, trailing
the fishnet of darkness in his wake.

There
I was. In bygone days.
The new has never begun. I'm a man,
of one flesh with his wife,
raising his children
for an age without fear.

(March 14, 1959)

FROM

Shadowland Rivers (1962)

Schattenland Ströme

1.

Der Adler

Mit gebreiteten Schwingen
über dem Strom,
über dem Moorwald steht
der Adler—im Wetterbogen
ein Zeichen mit schwelenden Rändern,
in das Holz meiner Tür
geschlagen, Krallen—ich werd
erwachen, taumelnd, am Waldberg
erwachen fliegenden Auges
aus dem Gesträuch.

Mit gebreiteten Schwingen,
den Adler hab ich genagelt
meinem Haus an den First—ich werd
schlafen, im Schlaf
fahren, ein Aschenzeichen,
über den Wäldern.

1.
The Eagle

With its wings outspread
over marshwood and stream,
the eagle hovers—a sign
in the rainbow, its vanes
ablaze, its talons gouged
into my door—
I shall awake, startled,
on the wooded hill,
I shall awake, eyes darting up
from the shrubs.

With its wings outspread
I've nailed the eagle
to the ridge of my roof—
I shall sleep, take to the air
in my sleep, a daub of ash
on the brow of the woods.

(July 20, 1960)

Ebene

See.
Der See.
Versunken
die Ufer. Unter der Wolke
der Kranich. Weiß, aufleuchtend
der Hirtenvölker
Jahrtausende. Mit dem Wind

kam ich herauf den Berg.
Hier werd ich leben. Ein Jäger
war ich, einfing mich
aber das Gras.

Lehr mich reden, Gras,
lehr mich tot sein und hören,
lange, und reden, Stein,
lehr du mich bleiben, Wasser,
frag mir, und Wind, nicht nach.

Plain

Lake.
The lake.
Its shores
sunken. Under the cloud,
the crane. White, lighting up
millennia
of herdsmen. With the wind

I climbed the mountain.
Here I'll reside. A hunter
I was, until caught up
in the grass.

Grass, teach me to speak,
teach me to be dead, to listen
at length, to speak. Stone,
teach me to endure, water,
and wind, ask not after me.

(June 20, 1960)

Rufe

Über dem breiten Hang—
der Wiese, den Zäunen, über
den Pfählen—ich war der Wind
und unablässige Rede
drunten des Stroms, ich kam
mit Kalmushänden, ich war
ohne Laut, ich lag
im Gras mit geöffneter Schläfe,
die Grillen umschnürten
mein Haar.

Einer, immer, der
nimmt mich auf, der ist
geflogen über den Winden, der hat
gehört auf die Rede
im Ufersand, wo die Kälte
brennt, auf dein Auge
legte sich Reif, einer Blume
schweigendes Eis, eine Träne
im Mittag.

Der
hat mich gehört. Ich sah nicht
den Mann, der die Angel
stellte tiefer, die Frauen
spülten die Wäsche vom Kahn,
es kam auf der Uferstraße
der andre mit Pferden, im Rauch,
über den Zäunen ging
der Gesang zweier Rufe, einer

Calls

Above the broad slope,
over the meadows, the fences,
above the poles, I was the wind
and the words, neverending,
of the river below, I came
with calamus hands, I was
soundless, I lay
in the grass, my temples
wide open, crickets
thick in my hair.

He who always lifts me up
has flown above the winds, has
listened to all the talk
in the sands of the shore,
where the cold
sears the hoarfrost
into your eye, a flower's
silent ice, a tear
at noon.

He has
heard me. I did not see
the man who lowered
his fishing rod, the women rinsing laundry
from the boat, or this other man
coming down the towpath
with his horse, in the smoke,
above the fences, the song of two voices
adrift, one bright

tönte hell und die Antwort
tief, sie verfing sich abends
aber im Wind.

of sound, the other deep
in answer, both caught up
in the evening wind.

(January 22, 1961)

Dryade

Birke, kühl
von Säften, Baum, der Atem
in meinen Händen, gespannt
Rinde, ein weiches Glas,
aber zu spüren tiefer
Regung, die Dehnung hinauf
im Stamm,
den Verzweigungen zu.

Laß,
in den Nacken hinab,
laß fallen dein Haar, ich hör
in meinen Händen, ich hör
durch die Kühle, ich hör ein Wehen,
hör anheben die Strömung,
steigende Flut,
den Taumel
singen im Ohr.

Dryad

Birch, cool
with sap, tree, your breath
in my hands, your bark
taut, lithe as glass,
yet to feel deeper
stirrings, the stretch
of the trunk
toward the branches.

Let
your hair fall down
upon your neck, I hear
in my hands, I hear
through the cool, I hear something
aflutter, I hear the river
rise, in my ear
I hear the thrum
of song.

(March 21, 1961)

Am Fluß

Himmel,
die Bläue, Bogen
alt, der mit uns
geht, den das Grün
bezaubert: Ufer, der schöne
Baum, auf dem Wasser sein Schatten,
der sich bewegt.

Da ist ein Streifen Rot,
eine Spur
Rot, wir sind es allein
zwischen Grün und Blau,
Himmel und Erde,
wann sagtest du:

"Es fliegen die Schatten, eine
Nacht hat gerufen
mit Käuzchenstimmen, das kam
unter den Bäumen heran,
der Himmel war fort"?

Jetzt,
der Himmel ist neu,
Atem, und keine Bläue,
es liegt deine Schläfe (ein Klopfen
langsam, nicht mehr zu hören,
nie mehr) auf meinem Mund.

At the River

Sky-
blue, this age-old
dome that goes with us,
enchanted
by the green: riverbank,
this lovely tree, its shadow
moving upon the waters.

Here, a strip of red,
a trace
of red, this is all we are,
between the green and the blue,
between heaven and earth,
when did you say:

"The shadows fly,
night called out
with owlet cries
beneath the trees
to vanish in the sky"?

Now
the sky is new,
breath, and no blue,
your temple at rest (a slow
throb, imperceptible)
upon my mouth.

(February 15, 1961)

Sommergeschrei

Kiebitz,
meinem Tag
fahr um die Kräuselstirn auf,
über das kurze
Horn, mit Schlingerflügen
über die Weide hinab
flieg, in den Brüchen
verflieg.

Breit, daß ich ertrink,
Leib, atmend, ich steh
mit erhobenen Armen, ich hab
gewartet, ich greif ein Gewölk, ich hab
gerufen, das hör ich, weit—

wo ich stand mit erhobenen
Armen, ich rührte
auf ein Gewölk.

Summer Cries

Lapwing,
fly over
my day's furrowed
brow, over shorthorn
steer, over pasture,
on lurching wing,
fly off
into the fens.

My girth at risk
of drowning, here I stand
and breathe with lifted arms, I've
waited, I grab at a cloud, I've
called, hear back, from afar

where I stood with lifted
arms, having managed to rouse
a cloud.

(November 18, 1960)

Ungesagt

Schwer,
ich wachse hinab,
Wurzeln
breite ich in den Grund,
die Wasser der Erde
finden mich, steigen,
Bitternis schmeck ich—du
bist ohne Erde,
ein Vogel den Lüften, leichter
immer im Licht,
nur meine Angst noch
hält dich
im irdischen Wind.

Unsaid

Heavy,
I grow downward,
I spread roots
into the ground,
the waters of the earth
find me, rise,
I taste the bitterness—you're
without earth,
bird of the air, ever lifted
into the light,
only my fear still
holds you
in the earthly wind.

(September 7, 1960)

Erzählung

Heller Sand, Spuren,
grün, und der fliegende Wald
Finsternis, hoch der stählerne Fisch
fährt durch die Bäume,
über die Wipfel auf, ich
setz nur den Schritt,
weiter den Schritt.

Kitesh, die Stadt,
hat Türme
und eine Straße,
dort steh ich,

augenlos erblicke ich dich,
ich tret auf dich zu
unhörbar,
ich rede dich an
ohne Stimme.

Tale

Bright sand, tracks,
green, and the forest dark
in flight, the steel fish
darts through the trees,
all I can do,
step by step,
is proceed.

The town of Kitezh
has towers
and a street,
there I stand,

eyeless, I see you,
out of earshot,
I approach you,
voiceless, to you
I speak.

(April 10, 1961)

Der Wanderer

Abends,
der Strom ertönt,
der schwere Atem der Wälder,
Himmel, beflogen
von schreienden Vögeln, Küsten
der Finsternis, alt,
darüber die Feuer der Sterne.

Menschlich hab ich gelebt,
zu zählen vergessen die Tore,
die offenen. An die verschloßnen
hab ich gepocht.

Jedes Tor ist offen.
Der Rufer steht mit gebreiteten
Armen. So tritt an den Tisch.
Rede: Die Wälder tönen,
den eratmenden Strom
durchfliegen die Fische, der Himmel
zittert von Feuern.

The Wanderer

Evenings,
river sounds,
woods' heavy breath,
sky filled
with shrieking birds, dark
cloud banks, ancient,
star-fire above.

I have lived like a man,
forgetting to count the open
doors, having always knocked
at those that were closed.

Every door is open.
The host stands with outspread
arms: Come to the table.
Say your piece: The woods
are full of sounds, the fish fly
through the river's breath,
the sky's aflicker with fires.

(July 25, 1960)

Wintergeschrei

Krähen, Krähen,
grünes Eis, Krähen
über dem Strom. Erstarrt
Gesträuch, seine Flucht
uferhinauf.

Schnee, er stäubt nicht,
wenn ihn dein Flügel streift,
Vogel, Strauchvogel, aber
ein wenig Blut
dein Herz
mitten im Eis, dein Ruf
eine Rauchspur über
der Sandbank,

wo unermüdend waren
Umarmungen, immer
lebte der Strom.

Winter Cries

Crows, crows,
green ice, crows
over the river. The bushes
frozen, retreating
up the banks.

The snow does not powder
when brushed by your wing,
bird, bird in the bush, but
a bit of blood,
your heart
iced up, your call
a wisp of smoke
over the sandbank,

where the embraces
went on forever, the river
always survived.

(November 3, 1959)

Tod des Wolfs

Zwischen Wald und Strom—
aber es ist
Nacht, unter dem Mond
Wölfe, die langen Schatten,
fort. Doch mein Eber kommt
starken Herzens, ein Bauer,
erntelustig,
auf seinem Feld.

Herbst,
mit den Nebeln
verflieg. Vor die hohe Wand
hingeduckt nun finstre
Zeit, vor das Eis, die Eulen
fahren über dem Schnee,
die Dämmerung fauchend,
ein Segel, verloren,
aus Schlaf.

Aber zerbrochen. Der Weg
hat eine Spur vom Gehöft
her. Da kam ich,
über die Schulter die Axt.
Vor der Wehe
lag der Wolf, eingefallen,
die Weiche zerpflügt.

Schweinchen, sag ich, tapferes
Schweinchen, dem Bösen hast
heimgezahlt. Dein Schnaufen,

The Death of the Wolf

Between wood and river—
but it's
night, beneath the moon,
wolves, their shadows long
gone. But here comes my boar,
stout-hearted peasant
eager to reap
his field.

Autumn,
fly off with your fogs.
The season of darkness
now crouches before the wall,
before the ice, the owls
swoop over the snow
and seethe at the dawn,
lost sails
of sleep.

But broken. There were tracks
on the farm road I took,
ax on my shoulder.
The wolf lay
by the snowdrift,
disemboweled,
flanks raked apart.

Pig, I say, brave little
pig, you pay
a pretty price. I'm so glad

fröhlich hör ichs,
es macht mir im Dunkel
warm.

to hear you snorting,
it warms me
in the dark.

(November 28, 1960)

Hamann

Das
eine Welt,
Straßen, Wege, heute
kommt der Wasianski, wer hat
die Lebensläufe geschrieben
und wer die Gedichte à la Grécourt,
zwischen Lizentgraben und
Katzbach alles, was weiß ich, Welt.

Über Nacht aber singt
in den zu stark verschnittenen
Bäumen ein Vogel,
sommerlang dieser Vogel,
er weckt mir den Sohn
nicht, aber ich—so werd ich
gehn, ich fisch ein Gericht
Irrlichter in den Wiesen
hinter dem Graben.

Welt. Ich seh im Regen
weiß ein Gewölk. Ich bin's.
Auf dem Pregel hinab
der Kahn. Aus den Nebeln. Welt.
Eine Hölle, da Gott inwohnt.
Welt. Ich sag mit Sancho:
Gott, ich sag: er versteht mich.

Hamann

That
entire world
of streets and lanes, today
Wasianski's slated to arrive, along with the author
of *The Lives* and the composer of
Poems à la Grécourt,
between Lizentgraben and
Katzbach, all this, I suppose, a world.

In the cruelly cropped trees
there's this bird that sings
the whole night through
all summer long, it
never wakes my son,
whereas I, I suppose I'll have to go
fish a dish of will-o'-the-wisps
in the meadows
beyond the ditch.

World. I see a white
cloud in the rain. It's me.
The skiff, down the Pregel.
Out of the mists. A world.
A hell, indwelt by God.
World. With Sancho I repeat:
God, I say, understands me.

(October 17, 1960)

Holunderblüte

Es kommt
Babel, Isaak.
Er sagt: Bei dem Pogrom,
als ich Kind war,
meiner Taube
riß man den Kopf ab.

Häuser in hölzerner Straße,
mit Zäunen, darüber Holunder.
Weiß gescheuert die Schwelle,
die kleine Treppe hinab—
Damals, weißt du,
die Blutspur.

Leute, ihr redet: Vergessen—
Es kommen die jungen Menschen,
ihr Lachen wie Büsche Holunders.
Leute, es möcht der Holunder
sterben
an eurer Vergeßlichkeit.

Elder Blossom

Here comes
Babel, Isaac.
He says: During the pogrom
when I was a child,
they tore the head off
my dove.

Houses along a wooden street,
fences, elders above.
The doorsill scrubbed white,
the small steps downward—
Then, you remember,
the flecks of blood.

People, you say: Forget it—
Here come the young,
their laughter like elder shrubs.
People, the elder could very well
die
of your forgetting.

(September 15, 1960)

An den Chassid Barkan

Als wir sangen, kamst du,
botest den Gruß, nach den Schwalben
sahst du. Wir hörten im Schatten
mittags den Alten,
ihren Seufzern und Flüchen zu.

Über den Berg
kamst du. So kamen immer
eure Männer, umwachsen
wie mit den Bärten eisern
mit ihren Namen, aber
die Locke leicht und die Füße
heiter, im Tanz, vom brennenden
Dornbusch, von einem Strom
(an den Weiden hingen die Harfen).

Geh nicht fort. Die Zeit
kommt auf, deine Pfade zu lieben,
inne zu werden des tiefen
Dunkels um Wälder und Ströme,
auszusäen mit Tränen,
zu ernten fröhlich.

To Barkan the Hassid

As we were singing, you came
to greet us, watching
the swallows. In the noonday
shade, we listened to the old men
sigh and complain.

You came from
beyond the mountains, as your men
always came, equipped with beards
and names, but light of curl and foot,
dancing away from the burning bush
and from the river (where the harps
hung from the willow trees).

Do not leave. The time
shall come to value your paths,
to take in the dark
of these rivers and woods,
to sow in tears,
to reap in joy.

(June 10, 1960)

Gedenkblatt

Jahre,
Spinnenfäden,
die großen Spinnen, Jahre—
es sind die Zigeuner gezogen
mit Pferden den Lehmpfad. Der alte Zigahn
kam mit der Peitsche, die Frauen
standen im Hoftor, redend,
in aufgebogenen Armen
die Handvoll Glück.

Später blieben sie aus.
Da kamen die Würger mit bleiernen
Augen. Einmal, die Alte
oben im Dach
hat den Entschwundenen nachgefragt.

Hör den Regen strömen
über den Hang, sie gehn,
die keiner mehr sieht,
auf dem alten Lehmpfad,
eingehüllt in die stäubenden
Wasser, Windkronen der Fremde
über dein Schwarzhaar,
leicht.

Memorial Page

Years,
gossamer,
enormous spiders, years—
the Gypsies traveling down
the dirt road with their horses. The old Roma
brandishing his whip, the women
standing at the farm gate, chatting,
offering up a handful of good fortune
in their outstretched arms.

They later failed to appear.
Then came the stranglers with their leaden
eyes. At one point, the old woman
up in the attic
inquired after those who had vanished.

Listen to the rain
stream down the slope,
they make their way, who
shall be seen no more,
down the old dirt road,
cloaked in the river mists,
their black hair softly crowned
by alien winds.

(August 2, 1960)

Wetterzeichen

Mit dem Fluß hinab,
dem Wiesenfluß
und den wilden Gerüchen
der Wälder, redend
laut mit dem Sommerlicht
und den Vögeln
gegen den Abend, im Dunkel
den Fledermäusen—im Winkelflug
fuhren sie auf und hinab
um eine Scheuer mit kleinen
Drachenflügeln—redend
kam ich hierher, hier bin ich,

auf dem Sandberg, ins trockne Moos
setz ich den Fuß, den breiten
Himmel hab ich getragen,
die atmenden Lüfte, ich schwanke,
es ist ein Rauschen, ich hör
in der dröhnenden Finsternis,

hör auf den Fluß, er lag
über dem Sand, die Hände
führte der Wind ihm,
der Sommer kam

mit Ermattungen, mit
Blut in den Augen, zuckenden
Schläfen, den Mund voll Rost,

Weathersigns

Down the river,
the meadow river,
and the wild scents
of the woods, talking out loud
to the summer light

and to the birds
toward evening, the bats
in the dark zigzagging
around the barn with their tiny
dragon wings, I came here
talking all the while,
here I am

on the sand hill, setting foot
on dry moss, bearing all of heaven
on my shoulders and all the breathings
of the breeze and, bewildered,
I hear a roar, and in the drone
of the dark

I listen to the river, lying
on the sand, its hands
guided by the wind,
summer coming in

fatigued, with bloodshot
eyes and its head
throbbing, its mouth full of rust,

aber er führte die Hände
meinem Fluß, der den Feuern
geht im Schatten der Fische,
im Schatten des Schilfs entgegen,
im Schatten der Bäume—

Flamme, flieg, die Küsten
fahren einwärts ins Land,
lautlos, wehend von Dünen,
um das verlassene Meer
sinken die Steine—Feuer,
leg in den Sturm die Schwingen
wie Rauch, er trägt vor den Wettern
dich, vor der rasenden Stille,

eh die Himmel brechen,
die siedenden Wetter, zerbrochen
die Lüfte dann, auf dem Sand
reglos der Fluß

und der Hügel getroffen,
ich halt einen Baum, ich red noch:
Wir sahen kommen die Zeichen
und schwinden, her durch die Stille
zwei Federn fielen herab.

yet guiding the hands
of my river as it rushes
toward the fires in the shadows
of the fish, in the shadows
of the reeds, in the shadows of the trees—

Flame, fly away, the coasts
drive inward to the plain,
soundless, blown from the dunes,
the stones sink into the forsaken sea—Fire,
set your wings like smoke
against the storm, they shall carry you
before the weather,
before the raging stillness,

before the heavens break
into squalls and the breezes
shatter, leaving the river
prone on the sand

and the hills laid low,
I hold on to a tree, still saying:
We saw the signs come
and go. Two feathers
spiraled through the stillness.

(November 23, 1960)

2.
Nänie

Stimmen, der Wind
über die Bucht
kommt, Rohrwerke, Helsingör
hat so getönt: über dem Sund
die Küste, gestreckt
gegen den Himmel, dort
auf dem Absturz steht,
der mich gerufen hat,
Helios, breiten Mundes,
unter dem Augenbogen
dunkel—die Feuer um ihn
um Schulter und Haar, die rasselnden
Züge, erbrausend: Planeten,
der mörderische
concentus der Welt.

Über der Bucht,
weit,
über dem Regen
farbenstrahlend aus Nebeln
der Bogen—Frieden
ist uns versprochen.

2.
Nänie

Voices, the wind
driving in
from the bay, organ pipes, thus
the sounds of Helsingør: over the stretch
of the far coast, against the sky, there
on the headland
he looms
who called out to me,
Helios, broad of mouth, dark
of eye, flames
about his shoulders and hair,
features ragged, racing by:
planets,
the murderous
concentus of the world.

Beyond the bay,
far off,
beyond the rain,
sifted through
the rainbow mist—Peace
promised us.

(October 11, 1960)

Seestück

Bleib,
Möwengeschrei,
wenn die Sonne verfiel—
die wir liebten, die Schwalbe
kam nun nicht mehr.
Tief, von Hageln zerschossen,
der Winter,
alt.

Bist du geblieben,
ein Freund mit der leisen Rede,
mit Händen
leicht?—wir hörten den Lüftezug
und die Dämmrung, ich hab
ein Wasser getrunken.

Bald,
mit brennenden Segeln,
ich fahr, Bootes zur Rechten,
zu Häupten den Schwan,—
windlos, Nacht, ich fahr,
Schattengestalt.

Seascape

Tarry
awhile, gull cry,
when the sun went dark
and our beloved swallows
no longer returned.
Deep, riddled with hail,
age-old,
winter.

Have you tarried awhile,
soft-spoken friend,
so light
of hand? We heard the rush of the breeze
at dusk, and I've taken a drink
of water.

Soon,
sails on fire,
I'll set off, Boötes to my right,
the Swan overhead—
windless, night, phantom
on his way.

(July 15, 1960)

Französisches Dorf

Martin,
in einer Wolke
weißer gewichtiger Vögel,
der Heilige kommt, und das Jahr,
unter dem harten Ahorn das Jahr
geht aus.

Wenn es dunkelt,
die singende Stille
lebt, ein redendes Wasser, ein halber Ruf
hinter dem Haus mit dem Zeichen,
windbeflogen das Hirtengespräch.

Ach, wenn das Jahr
dunkelt, wenn ich die Wetterfahn'
kreisen seh, die Zeit nach ihr zähl—
hiß, Angélique, den Sommer,
den roten Rode, aus dem höchsten
Fenster schrei mich ins Licht!

French Village

Here comes Martin
in a cloud
of white majestic geese,
here comes the saint,
and there goes the year
in a swirl of maple leaves.

When darkness falls,
the singing stillness
comes alive, the half call of the water
behind church and cross,
shepherds' talk, windblown.

Ah, when the year
darkens, when I see the weathervanes
whirl and count time by their turn—
hike up, Angélique, your red skirt
of summer, from your window on high
shout me into the light!

(December 19, 1958)

Brentano in Aschaffenburg

Zeichen.
Ein Pfirsichbaum
in die Gitter geflochten
unter der Mauer. So bröckelt
heller der Stein.

Ach ein Blatt
gegen die Röte umher:
Mauer, Kirche und Gartenhaus.
Treppen. Die Straße hinab.
Draußen die Wiesen.

Kühl. Lüfte aus Grün.
Vor den offenen Himmel
gebettet der Strom. Im fallenden
Wind das Geheul.
—
"Weh, ohn Opfer..."
Der Staub auf der Stiege
rötlich, es kommt ein Mann,
dick, die Hand auf dem Herzen,
er schließt an der eichenen Tür.

Brentano in Aschaffenburg

Signs.
A peach tree
atwist in the trellis
beneath the wall. Thus the sandstone
crumbles more brightly.

Ah, a leaf here
against the reds:
wall, church, garden house.
Steps. Down the street.
The meadows beyond.

Cool. Wafts of green.
The stream bedded
under the open sky. In the dying
wind, the howls.
—
"Alas, without sacrifice..."
The dust on the stairs,
reddish, a man appears,
fat, hand upon his heart,
to unlock the oaken door.

(December 31, 1960)

Hölderlin in Tübingen

Bäume irdisch, und Licht,
darin der Kahn steht, gerufen,
die Ruderstange gegen das Ufer, die schöne
Neigung, vor dieser Tür
ging der Schatten, der ist
gefallen auf einen Fluß
Neckar, der grün war, Neckar,
hinausgegangen
um Wiesen und Uferweiden.

Turm,
daß er bewohnbar
sei wie ein Tag, der Mauern
Schwere, die Schwere
gegen das Grün,
Bäume und Wasser, zu wiegen
beides in einer Hand:
es läutet die Glocke herab
über die Dächer, die Uhr
rührt sich zum Drehn
der eisernen Fahnen.

Hölderlin in Tübingen

Trees, earthbound, the lie of the light
upon the boat, oars laid out
on the bank, gently summoned
by the shade
that passed before this door
then trailed along a river,
the Neckar, the green Neckar,
winding around meadows,
willows on its shore.

Tower,
that it provide a home
as viable as day, the heft
of its walls, massed
against the green
water and trees, to weigh
both in a single hand,
the church bell echoing
over the roofs, the clock
inching forward to the creak
of the weathervanes.

(May 30, 1961)

Nachtschwalben

1.
Kalt,
die durchspeerte Luft,
das Schwarz und das Weiß, Licht, redend
auf Vogelstraßen. Der Abend, sein Stierhorn
schräg im Feuerrauch auf dem Horizont. Du sahst
steigen den Fisch, als die Wasser
klirrten, von meinen Augen
nahmst du die Hand, uns umflog
Schwärze und ohne Flügel
und ohne Schrei.

2.
Wir atmeten,
das Dach auf meiner Schulter
war leicht und wie ein Regen
himmellos
die Nadelstreu im Sand,
Nachtschwalben, Seelen,
wo Schatten war,
dicht auf der Erde,
kalt.

Night Swallows

1\.
Cold
stabs the air,
black and white, the light speaks out
along bird routes. Horizon smoke
gored by night. You saw
the fish strike, as the waters
roiled, and took my hand
from my eyes, surrounded
by the black, without wing,
without cry.

2\.
We breathed.
The roof lay light upon my shoulders
and like some skyless
rain
the needles spattered the sand,
night swallows, souls,
where shadow stood
thick and cold
upon the ground.

(May 11, 1961)

Von den Strömen

Ce n'était pas assez que tant de mers, ce n'était pas assez que tant de terres eussent dispersé la course de nos ans.
—Saint-John Perse

Von den Strömen
gekommen der See, gegangen
durch Zähne und Klauen, Brandung,
Küsten, diese Wälder aus zitternder Luft—
aufgerichtet ist
mit faltigem Rückenfell
die hohe Ebene, bräunlich
mit Schründen, Abstürzen—hier
ist eine Wolke die Zeit,
groß, gestiegen über
den Himmel und reine Lüfte
trinkend, atmend
die Regen des Lichts.

Inseln immer, das weißt du,
über den Wassern, über
der Ferne, dort bist du geboren,
schwankend, dort bist du geboren,
zu einer Zeit, die ein Vogel
war, gefiedert mit zahllosen
Farben zwischen
Ocker und Rosa, es war
ein Vogel, du weißt.

Aber du tratst vor die Ebene,
die Gebirge herauf
bist du gegangen hinter den Trägern, du tratst
vor den Schlaf, vor die Ebene,

Of Rivers

Ce n'était pas assez que tant de mers, ce n'était pas assez que tant de terres eussent dispersé la course de nos ans.
—Saint-John Perse

From the rivers
comes the lake, having traveled
through tooth and claw and surf
and coast, these woods of quivering air—
the high plain
rucked up like a wrinkled
hide, brownish
rifts and cliffs—here
time is a cloud,
huge, risen
above the sky, drinking in
fresh breezes, inhaling
downpours of light.

Islands always, you know well,
across the waters, across
the distances, there you were born,
wavering, there you were born
at a time that was a bird,
feathered with countless
hues, between
ocher and pink, a bird
for sure, you know well.

But you stood before the plain,
you climbed mountains
behind your porters, you stood
before sleep, before the plain

die unter weißen Lidern
erwachte, zu eines grünen
Tieres Gesang, des Bewohners
fliegender Wälder, der
seine Flügel nicht weiß.

Dort
leb, deine Augen gehn
über der See, eine Strömung,
weiß, noch wenn es dunkelt
weiß, ohne Heftigkeit, dicht
unter das Herz gelagert,
redend, Finsternis, aus
Stimmen die Segel, gehalten
von Männern mit Federhemden
und roten Haarschöpfen, abends,

unter dem Wind.

as it awoke, opening its white lids
to the song
of a green forest creature
in flight, unaware
of its wings.

Settle
there, your eyes taking in
the waves, the riptides,
white, even as the dark descends,
white, without insistence, well-
housed within the heart, primed for
speech, dark, the sails
full of voices, manned
by sailors in feathery shirts
and shocks of red hair, evenings,

windward isles.

(December 19, 1960)

Vogelstraßen 1957

1.
Im Regen schlief ich,
im Regenröhricht erwacht ich.
Eh es blättert, seh ich den nahen Mond,
hör ich den Zugvogelschrei,
den Lufterschüttrer, den weißen
Schrei, der die Luft zerschlägt.

Schnell und scharf
wie die Wölfe wittern,
Schwester, lausch! Wäinemöinen
singt durch den Wind,
wirft aus Schnee den Fittich
auf deine Schulter, wir treiben
flügelnd im Liederwind—

2.
aber unter großen
Himmeln allein, verlassne
Straßen der gefiederten
Heere, die vergingen—
schlafend auf den Winden
fuhren sie, eine neue
Sonne flammte, die Lohe
schlug herauf, sie brannten
im Aschenbaum.

Dort sind aufgeflogen
unsere Lieder auch.
Schwester, deine Hände

Bird Routes 1957

1.
I slept in the rain
and woke in the dripping reeds.
Before the leaves fall, I see the nearby moon,
I hear the migrating birds
break the breeze with their white
shrieks, shattering the air.

Swift and sharp
as the sniff of wolves,
sister, take heed! Väinämöinen
sings through the wind,
drapes a pinion of snow
upon your shoulder, amid flights
of song we drift on wings—

2.
but alone under
the immense skies, under
the deserted routes
of all those vanished feathered troops
who dozed off while driven
by the winds, a new sun
flares forth, the bark
scorched, incinerated
in the ash tree.

There our songs
also took wing. Sister, your hands
grow pale, you sleep your way

bleichen, du schläfst mir im Dunkel
fort—wann soll ich
singen der Vögel Angst?

away from me in the dark—
when shall I sing of the terror
that gripped the birds?

(September 1957)

Gertrud Kolmar

Buche, blutig im Laub,
in rauchender Tiefe, bitter
die Schatten, droben das Tor
aus Elstergeschrei.

Dort ist eine gegangen,
Mädchen, mit glattem Haar,
die Ebene unter den Lidern
lugte herauf, in den Mooren
vertropfte der Schritt.

Ungestorben aber
die finstere Zeit, umher
geht meine Sprache und ist
rostig von Blut.

Wenn ich deiner gedächte:
Vor die Buche trat ich,
ich hab befohlen der Elster:
Schweig, es kommen, die hier
waren—wenn ich gedächte:
Wir werden nicht sterben, wir werden
mit Türmen gegürtet sein?

Gertrud Kolmar

Beech, bloody of leaf,
deep in smoke, bitter
the shadows, above the gate,
magpie screams.

There walked a girl
with silken hair,
the plain under her lids
glanced up, her every step
seeped into the marshes.

But the dark times
have not died, my speech
strays, all
rusted up with blood.

To remember you,
I'd have stepped up to the beech tree
and told the magpie:
Hold your tongue, here they come
who once were here. To remember you:
"No, we shall not die, we shall be
girded about by towers!"

(January 9, 1961)

Else Lasker-Schüler

Windbruch
über die Erde
streu ich. Schwester. Jedes
ungestorbene Land
ist dein Grab.

Przemysl, Brzozów, wer
seine Stätte
aushob, ist
verscharrt. In Mielce das Haus
Gottes
brennend, über die Flammen
hinauf die Stimme, eine
Stimme, aber
aus hundert Mündern, aus
der Erstickung. Wie sagt
man: im Feuerofen
erhob sich das Lob
Gottes—wie sagt
man?

Ich weiß
nicht mehr.
Über die Erde, Schwester,
Windbruch, ausgestreut. Wie
Bäume verkrallt
Gesehenes in
den Schatten mittags, in
die Dämmerung unter den Schwingen
der Vögel, in
das Eis, in

Else Lasker-Schüler

I scatter
wind-torn branches
over the earth. Sister. Each
undying land
your tomb.

Przemysł, Brzozów, whosoever
dug his own grave
now lies in it,
sprawled. In Mielec
the house of God
on fire, above the flames
a voice, the voice
of hundreds of mouths,
arising
from suffocation. How say
this: out of the furnaces
emerged praise
of God—how say
this?

I no longer
know.
Over the earth, sister,
wind-torn branches,
scattered. Like
trees, what is seen
clings to the midday
shade, at dusk
under the wings
of birds, in

die Ödnis
nachts.

Liebe
(du sprichst aus dem Grab)
Liebe tritt, eine weiße
Gestalt,
aus der Mitte des Grauens.

the icy wastes
of night.

Love,
(you speak from the grave)
Love, step forth, a figure
in white,
from the pit of horror.

(August 25, 1960)

An Nelly Sachs

Die Tiere haben Höhlen und die Vögel
unter dem Himmel haben Nester

Höhlen, das Waldgetier
fährt hinab,
und der versengt und geschwemmt
war, der Holzpfahl Perun,
in die Erde auch
ist er gegangen, unter
den Dnjepr, so schreit noch aus
der Strom seine Rede: Kommt
von zerbrochnen Gehölzen, Tiere
kommt, das Getier hat Höhlen.

Der die Himmel trägt,
über Türmen
steht er des Lichts, für ihn
ist der Baum, seine Brut
unter den Flügeln, Schatten
nährt ihn und Regen, die Vögel,
die eiligen Herzen,
haben ein Nest.

(Hoch, ein Aufschein, der Adler
zog, in den Fängen
die schreiende Nachtigall, über
der Brandstatt riefen die Schwalben—
der Bewohner der Höhle
fiel auf die Erdwand, Sand
um die Schläfe strich er,
die Wurzeln fraßen
Gesicht und Gehör.)

To Nelly Sachs

Foxes have holes and birds in the air
have nests

Holes, into which the foxes
retreat,
and where, flayed and drowned,
the wooden idol of the god Perun
is also gone
unto the earth, beneath
the Dnieper, his cry still rising
from the waves: Leave
your broken groves. Come
foxes, for you have holes.

Who upholds the heavens
commands
towers of light, the tree
is his, his brood
beneath his wings, fed
by shadow and rain, his birds,
quick of heart,
have a nest.

(High, in an upward flash,
the eagle soared, the shrieking
nightingale in his talons,
the swallows calling out
over the scorched earth,
the fox falling against the wall
of soil, sand smeared against his snout,
the roots devouring
all he saw or heard.)

Wer hat, daß er sein Haupt
lege, der wird
schlafen, hören aus Träumen
in einen Schrei, der die Ebenen
abfliegt, über Gewässern
fliegt—ein Licht kam, zwei Hügel
bogs auseinander, erkennbar
der Pfad, die Steine, Ufer,
grün vor Glanz—der Schrei
lautlos, "Löwenzahns Samen,

nur beflügelt mit Gebeten".

Who has a place
to lay his head, shall
sleep, shall hear
in his dreams a cry
soaring over the plains
and waters—and there was light,
parting the two hills,
the paths, stones, riverbanks
recognizable, glints of green—the cry
soundless, "Dandelion seeds,

yet winged with prayer."

(June 19, 1961)

3.
Der Don

Hoch, aus Feuern
die Dörfer. Über den Fels
fallen die Ufer. Aber
der Strom gefangen, Eishauch
wehte er, Stille finster
folgte ihm nach.

Weiß war der Strom. Das höhere
Ufer dunkel. Die Pferde
stiegen den Hang auf. Einmal,
die Ufer drüben
flogen davon, wir sahn
hinter den Feldern, weit,
unter dem Frühmond, Mauern
gegen den Himmel.

Dort
singt der Diw,
im Turm,
er schreit an die Wolke, der Vogel
ganz aus Unglück, er ruft
über die Felsenufer,
befiehlt zu hören den Ebenen.
Hügel, öffnet euch, sagt er,
tretet hervor gerüstet,
Tote, legt an den Helm.

3.
The Don

On high, the villages
of fire. The banks fall
across the rock. But the river,
imprisoned, a breath
of ice, followed by
the voiceless dark.

The river was white. The upper
bank dim. The horses
climbed its slope. Once
the opposite shores
fell away, we saw
behind the fields, far
below the early moon, walls
against the sky.

There
sings the Div,
crying out to the cloud
from the tower, the bird
of ill omen calling
over the rocky banks,
commanding the plains to listen.
All you hills, open wide, says the Div,
all you dead, step forth in your mail,
helmets on your skulls.

(August 3, 1960)

Ikone

Türme, gebogen, verzäunt
von Kreuzen, rot. Finster
atmet der Himmel, Joann
steht auf dem Hügel, die Stadt
gegen den Fluß. Er sieht
kommen das Meer mit Balken,
Rudern, räudigen
Fischen, der Wald
wirft sich herab in den Sand.
Her vor dem Wind
geht der Fürst, er schwenkt
Fackeln in beiden Händen, er streut
lautlose Feuer
über die Ebenen aus.

Icons

Towers, leaning, fenced off
with crosses, red. The sky draws
a dark breath, Joanne
stands upon the hill, the town
overlooking the river. He watches
the sea sweep in with all its planks
and oars and mangy
fish, as the forest
hurtles into the sand.
The prince strides
before the wind, brandishing
torches in both hands, sowing
silent fires
across the plains.

(October 27, 1960)

Verlassene Ortschaft

Über den Markt,
der leer ist, mit Hühnerflügeln
der Wind
zieht eine Spur in den Staub.

Zäune. Schräggesunken
Kreuze. Die Dohlenstimme.
Wer kommt, ein Brett auf der Schulter,
wer will das neue Sims
für die Fenster schneiden, wer
kam, einen grünen Topf
unter dem Schultertuch?

Hier geht niemand. Der Himmel
findet ein Band
liegen und hebt es auf,
die Hauswand bewächst
Moos, Nebel umfliegt
einen weißen Turm, und woher
bist du gekommen?

Über klirrende Drähte
der Weidegärten, über
die Wiese am Moorloch, Wasser
folgt dir, es füllt deine Spuren schwarz.

Deserted Village

Over the empty marketplace
the wind traces
tracks in the dust with chicken
wings.

Fences. Crosses askew
in the soil. The voice of the jackdaw.
Who shall come, a wooden plank
upon his shoulder, who shall saw
a new windowsill, who
came, a green pot
under his shawl?

Here no one goes. The sky
finds a ribbon lying there
and lifts it into the air, moss
grows on the house wall,
fog enshrouds
a white tower, and from where
have you come?

Across the clatter of wire
on the pasture fence, across the meadow
by the boghole, the water
follows you. Its black fills your foot tracks.

(February 5, 1961)

Unter dem Nachtrand

Unter dem Nachtrand die kleinen
Städte im Wind, aus verwirrten
Dächern, gilbenden Wänden,
Getürm. Die versinken im Land.

Zelte, mürb, vor dem Himmel,
vom Nachhall gestorbener Stimmen,
zerrissener Glockenmünder
verhängt und frierend vor Alter.

Und die Ebene geht
durch ihre Gassen, auf Plätzen
weilend vor den geöffneten
Türen und über den Brunnen.

Nachts aber ist's: sie fahren
Ströme hinab, in der starren
Waldung der Maste Segel,
feucht, bemalte, blätternde
Fahnen. Ich kam

unter dem Nachtrand, draußen
kauerte, ehe der Wald
anhob, ein Dorf, der Zigeunerin
gleich, der Dunklen, im Lichtschein
schwang sie das Pfännlein über
zerstiebendem Feuer, der Rauch
zog ihren Scheitel.

Under the Edge of Night

Under the edge of night, small
villages in the wind, jumble
of roofs, yellowing walls,
towers. All sink into the plain.

Scrim of tents against the sky
echoing with dead voices,
cracked mouths of bells
sodden and frozen with age.

And the plain streams
through their streets, pausing
in squares, above the fountains,
before open doors.

It's night: they travel down
the rivers in a stiff
forest of masts, sails
damp, painted pennants
like leaves. I arrived

under the edge of night, a village
squatted there, before
the woods, like a dark Gypsy
woman waving her small pan
over the dying fire,
the smoke parting
her hair.

(July 1952)

Nordrussische Stadt
(Pustoschka 1941)

Falb
an die Straße nach Norden
gefallen der Bergwall. Die Brücke,
das alte Holz,
im Ufergesträuch.

Da lebt der Fluß,
weiß im Geröll, über dem Sand
blind. Und Krähengeschrei
sagt deinen Namen: Wind
um ein Gebälk, ein Rauch
gegen den Abend.

Der kommt,
Geleucht inmitten
der Wolke, er folgt den Winden,
er späht nach dem Feuer aus.

Fern entbrennts
in der Ebene,
weit. Die an Wäldern
wohnen, auf Flüssen, im hölzernen
Glück der Dörfer, abends,
lauschen, legen
das Ohr an die Erd.

North Russian Town
(Pustoschka 1941)

Dun,
on the road northward
the rampart has collapsed. The bridge,
the old woodpiles
in the bushy banks.

This is where the river lives,
white among the pebbles, blind
upon the sands. The crow's caw
says your name: wind
in the rafters, evening
smoke.

Here it comes,
a brightness between
the clouds, after the winds,
scouting the fire.

It burns out far
in the plains.
Those who live
along the rivers,
among the forests, in the wooden
contentment of their village homes,
lend an ear to the earth, at eventide.

(September 1956)

Aufenthalt

Keiner erfährt, wo wir waren,
mit trüben Augen Hunde
sahen uns laufen hinab
an Zäunen, schwarz das Haus
und das Land um die Wolgaquelle
hügelig, Haus und Wand,
verblichen das Bild:

Tolstoi, alt, an den Balken
gereckt der hölzernen Bahnstation,
bäurisch mit den Händen,
erschreckenden, die zu schmal sind
für ein Gered im gestirnten Schloß,

wo der Schatten vorbeischleift
an den Zäunen—ich kenne
die Gräber nicht, er entstieg
Grüften aber, ich weiß,
ich lehn mich ins Licht, das die Berge
befällt mit der Wildnis der Lüfte—
Vogelzüge, Geschrei
drübenher, über mir, dort
in die Ferne davon—ich stand
auf verschütteten Strömen,
hörte seufzen den Sand,
ich war ein hölzerner Schatten,
beschlagen mit Eisen, umflogen
vom fallenden Licht.

In Transit

No one knows where we were,
dogs with rheumy eyes
saw us run down
along the fence, the house black
and the countryside around the source of the Volga
hilly, the image of the house and its walls
now faded:

Old Tolstoy, lying there dying
on the planks of the wooden railway station,
brutish, his hands frightening,
too scrawny to engage in any more quarrels
with his starstruck estate,

where the shade slinks by
the fences—I have no knowledge
of the tombs, but I know
he climbed out of his grave,
I lean into the light, which falls
from the mountains with the wildness
of the wind, bird flight and bird cries
above me, behind me, there
in the distance, I stood on the spill
of streams, I heard the sigh
of the sands, I was a wooden
shade, banded with iron, besieged
by the dying light.

(March 17, 1961)

Über dem Strom

Sand,
kalt, lebendig
von Quellen, im Atem lautlos
geht er des Stroms, durch den See
folgend der Strömung, über
dem offenen Auge der Tiefe,
über dem Schlaf
scheint er ein Licht, von Flossen
glänzend, es ziehn in den Nebeln
die Vögel ihm nach.

Dann,
das Ufer wieder
empfängt ihn mit Händen
grün, mit der finsteren Erde
und dem Getier, das den Rücken zeigt.

Aber die Stadt
kommt, auf die Ufer gebogen
weiß, erschallend von Türmen,
Mauern im Krähenschatten
gegen den Abend, dem Gold
über den Firsten, die Stadt,
leise vom Lärm ihrer Kindheit,
den wehenden Frösten, dem Alter,
draußen dem Schnee.

Der den Himmel füllt,
Schnee, und die Leere hinter
der Röte, hinter den Feuern,
die Leere. Wind, mit den Vögeln

Above the River

Sand,
cold, alive
with springs, soundlessly
seeps through the river's
breath, following its currents
through the lake, over
the open eye of the deep,
over sleep,
like a light, aglint
with fins, followed by birds
in the mist.

Then
the shore again
welcomes it in with green
hands, its dark earth
and beasts showing their backs.

But the town
comes into view, a white bend
on the bank, full of the sounds
of towers and the shadows
of crows at dusk, gold
on the roof ridges, town
with its soft din of children,
and with age, frost-bound
by the snow of the steppes.

Snow that fills the sky
and the void
behind the reds, behind

fliegst du, so fall herab
über mein Segel, ich ruf dich,
Wind, ich seh die Ebenen
abgewandt, alt.

the fires. Wind, who soars
with the birds, fill
my sails, I call upon you,
wind, I see the plains,
turn away, old.

(October 5, 1960)

Kathedrale 1941

Die wir sahn
über dem Winterstrom,
über der Wasser reißender
Schwärze, Sophia, klingendes
Herz der verdüsterten Nowgorod—

Finster wars schon voreinst.
Doch mit schäumenden, heitren
Delphinen vorübergezogen
kam die Zeit, Fruchtgärten
brannten die Wange dir, oft
hinter den Zäunen hielten
Pilger nassen Gesichts
in deiner Kuppeln goldnem Geschrei.
Und deine Nacht, die Mondschlucht,
tödlich blaß, es erglänzte
der halkyonische Vogel
im Eisgenist.

Rauch hat dir die Wände
geschwärzt, deine Türen zerbrach
Feuer, wie wird sein
das Licht deinen Fensterhöhlen?
Alles an unsrem Leben
wars getan, der Schrei
wie das Schweigen, wir sahn
steigen über die Ebene,
weiß, dein Gesicht.

Cathedral 1941

Which we glimpsed
across the winter river,
across the black rush
of its waters, Sophia, resonant
heart of gloomy Novgorod—

long known for its dark.
Yet with the joyous leap and
splash of dolphins, the time came
for your cheeks to be seared
by orchards, pilgrims often
halted behind your fences,
faces in tears
at the golden cries of your domes.

And your night, the moon's rift
deathly pale, the halcyon bird
bright
in its nest of ice.

Smoke has blackened
your walls, fire has broken through
your doors, how shall the light stream
through your shattered windows?
All this was done
to our life, both the cries
and the silence, over the plains
we saw the white
of your face, rising.

Damals
in den Mooren,
draußen, ging auf
der Zorn.
Zorn, eine schwere Saat.
Wie will ich rufen
einmal
das Aug mir noch
hell?

Back then,
amid the marshes,
out there, the wrath
was unleashed.
Wrath, a heavy seed.
How shall I call out
one day,
my eyes
still bright?

(December 29, 1955)

Dorfkirche 1942

Rauch
um Schneedach und Balkenwand.
Über den Hang hinab
Krähenspuren. Aber der Fluß
im Eis.

Dort
Aufschein, zerstürzt
Stein, Gemäuer, der Bogen,
geborsten die Wand,

wo das Dorf stand
gegen den Hügel, der Fluß
sprang im frühen Jahr,
ein Lamm, vor der Tür,
eine runde Bucht
war für den Wind,

der auf den Höhen umher
geht, finster, der eigene
Schatten, er ruft, rauhstimmig
die Krähe
schreit ihm zurück.

Village Church 1942

Smoke
over the snowy roof and log walls.
Crow tracks down
the slope. And the river
iced over.

There
a burst of light, shattered
stone, debris, arch
and wall in ruin,

where the village stood
against the hill, in the new year
the river leapt,
a lamb before the door,
a stall provided
for the wind

roaming
the heights, dark
shadow of itself,
calling out
to the hoarse reply
of a crow.

(August 19, 1960)

Bericht

Bajla Gelblung,
entflohen in Warschau
einem Transport aus dem Ghetto,
das Mädchen
ist gegangen durch Wälder,
bewaffnet, die Partisanin
wurde ergriffen in Brest-Litowsk,
trug einen Militärmantel (polnisch),
wurde verhört von deutschen
Offizieren, es gibt
ein Foto, die Offiziere sind junge
Leute, tadellos uniformiert,
mit tadellosen Gesichtern,
ihre Haltung
ist einwandfrei.

Report

Bajla Gelblung,
a young girl
who escaped a transport
from the Warsaw ghetto
took to the woods and was captured
as an armed partisan in Brest-Litovsk
wearing a (Polish) military outfit
and interrogated
by German officers,
a photo survives,
all the officers young,
impeccably uniformed
with impeccable features,
their posture
flawless.

(January 17, 1961)

Kloster bei Nowgorod

Strom, schwer,
den die Lüfte umdrängen, alt,
Geister der tiefen
Ebene, redend im Regen
uferhinab. Der Hecht
steht unterm Schilf.

An dem weißen Gemäuer
Glockenschläge Licht,
über die Dächer sinkend
das Hungertuch Nacht, von verstummten
Vögeln durchstürzt.

Türen, leer, der steinerne
Pfad, auf verwachsener Stufe
der Greis mit dem weißen Scheitel,
wenn Gesang im ertönenden Bogen
aufsteht, Wind tritt ins erzene
Tor, silberner steigt,
flossenstarrend
der Hecht aus dem Grund.

Cloister near Novgorod

River, leaden,
besieged by the winds, old,
ghosts of the deep
plains, talking across the banks
in the rain. The pike
lies under the reeds.

Light on the white wall
like a tolling bell,
the Lenten veil of night
sinks over the roofs,
punctured by the silenced birds.

Doors, empty, the stone
path, on the overgrown step
the old monk with his shock of white hair,
when the chant reaches into the echoes
of the arches, the wind strides
through the iron gate, and the silvery
stiff-finned pike
rises to the surface.

(July 23, 1955)

Die Tomsker Straße

Schrei herüber, der Wind
schlägt in die Harfenstricke
—Tiergedärm, auf die Äste
der Birke gewunden, dort
gehen die Hügelrücken,
ich hör eine Harfe, hinter
dem Bahndamm, ich seh
aber die Straße nicht, Jelisaweta
sagte voreinst:

An der Tomsker Straße,
die Bauern stellten ins Fenster
Kwaß und Brot auf die Nacht,
der Fremdling kam,
schritt vorüber, keiner
sagte "Verbannter," "unglücklich"
hieß er, er hatte
hundert Namen, jeder
konnte ihn rufen.

So war die Straße, sagte
Jelisaweta, sie ging
in ein Land wie der Himmel,
einen Sommer, aufschäumt' er
von Blumen, die riesigen Bäume
trugen den Himmel, es kam
aber der Schnee, es kam
Jelisaweta nach Jahren,
die Brüder standen am Ufer,

The Road to Tomsk

A cry, the wind
plucking at the harp strings
of the entrails wound
around the branches of the mountain
birches, I hear
a harp behind
the embankment, I cannot
see the road. Yelizaveta
once said:

Along the road to Tomsk
at night the peasants used to set out
kvass and bread in their windows,
and a stranger might pass by
and no one would call him
an "exile" or "unlucky"—
he had hundreds of
names, by which anyone
could call him.

Such was the road, said
Yelizaveta, it led into a land
like Heaven, foaming with flowers
in the summer, its towering trees
upholding the skies, but then
the snows came, then
years later Yelizaveta came back,
her brothers were gathered on the shore,

der Enkel trat auf den Weg,
warf die Angel ins Gras.

and her grandson appeared upon the road
and tossed his fishing rod into the weeds.

(May 30, 1961)

Russische Lieder

Maryna
von einem Turm
über die Landschaft der Felsen hinab
singend, drei Flüsse
unter den Füßen ihr, aber
Nacht und des Winds
Schatten im Flug.

Schöne Geliebte,
mein Baum,
dir im Gezweig
hoch mit offener Schläfe
gegen den Mond
schlaf ich, begraben
in meine Flügel.

Schlaf ich—
du reichst mir ein Salzkorn,
geschöpft im unbefahrenen
Meer, ich geb dir wieder
einen Tropfen Regen
aus dem Lande,
wo keiner weint.

Russian Songs

Marina
sings from her tower
over the rocky landscape below,
three rivers at her feet, yet
within the wingbeat of night
and the flight of shadows
through the winds.

O my beloved,
my tree,
up in your branches,
my brow bared
to the moon,
I sleep, buried

in my wings.
I sleep—
you reach me a grain of salt,
product of some uncrossed sea,
and I give you back a drop
of rain from the land
where nobody
sheds a tear.

(September 26, 1960)

Gedächtnis für B.L.

Wenn das Dorf
tönt, atmendes Grün
um Sandweg und Steckenzaun,
wenn es geregnet hat,
Schwalbenflug, Himmel,
weiß, groß genug für den Regenbogen,
Abend, die Schläfe,
in die sich die Hand schmiegt, der Mund
singt ohne Laut.

Und
zu rufen nichts mehr.
Es fliegen die Sterne, rauschend,
mit Flügeln, dein Tod
fragt meinem Leben nach. Regen
(sag ich) und Grün, der Vogel
streifte den Bogen,
Licht stäubte auf, eine Wolke
Glanz, wir sahn ihn
nicht mehr.

In Memory of B.L.

When village sounds
fill the air, a breath of green upon
the sandy path and picket fence,
after the rain,
swallow flight, the sky
white, rainbow-wide,
evenings, knuckles
pressed against the brow, mouth
singing without a sound.

With
nothing left to be called.
The stars rush away
on wings, your death asks
questions of my life. Rain
(I insist) and greenery, the bird
grazing the rainbow, the light
filtering upward, a cloud
brightening, and we saw him
no more.

(May 31, 1960)

Die Furt

Durch die Wälder geschlungen,
ihr weißen Wege, im Mittag.
Einer fiel auf den grünen
Hang und dem Fluß zu,
trank vom Wasser der Furt.
Die Schwalbe flog auf.

Und ich weiß die Hütte
drüben in Kirschbäumen. Dort
bist du geschritten. Schilfflöten
tönten. Mitten im Schnee,
im Windfall
kehr ich zurück.

The Ford

White paths, winding your way
through the midday woods,
one of you led down the green slope
toward the river, to drink
of the waters by the ford.
The swallow shot up.

And I know that hut
over there in the cherry trees. There
you used to walk to the panpipes
of the reeds. Amid the snow,
across the wind-torn branches,
I shall return.

(May 2, 1956)

Holzhaus

Jung,
aus weißer Fichte
damals das Haus—
lebendig im fließenden Harz,
redend die Nacht durch,
Balken und Bretter umsaust
von Träumen, geflügelten, weich
unter den Kiefern, lautlos
flogen die Eulen.

Rindenlos
in den Wettern
bliebst du, in langen Regen,
Fröste krallten
sich ein in die Tür. Du bist
alt zum Weinen. So kehren
wir alle zurück, wir tragen
unsere Toten unter dein Dach.

Du mit dem Mond
und den Winden vom Sommer hebst
auf dein Gesicht, es ist hell—
so scheint in der Mädchen Antlitz
die harte Schönheit der Liebe.

Haus,
einst, wenn du uns stirbst,
fällt zusammen alles,
Wände und Dach und Herd
fallen, die Liebe stürzt

Wooden House

Back then
when the white pine
house was still young—
talking the whole night through,
flowing with sap, beams and rafters
crowded with dreams,
wingèd ones, owls
sweeping their soft soundless way
beneath the pines.

Stripped of bark,
you withstood the storms
during the long freezing rains
as the frosts clawed
their way indoors. You are too old
for tears. Thus we all
make our return, bearing
our dead beneath your roof.

You with the moon
and summer winds upon your face,
it's now bright as day—that instant when
a young girl's features take on
the fierce beauty of love.

House,
when it comes time for you to die,
everything falls apart,
walls and roof and hearth,
the way love

so—ihr Knistern, wie dunkelts,
ihre Stätte
kennt sie nicht mehr.

dies—its fierce fire
gone dark, its former residence
unknown.

(December 30, 1957)

Heimweg

Blau.
Die Lüfte.
Der hohe Baum,
den der Reiher umfliegt.
Und das Haus,
einst, wo nun der Wald
herabkommt,
klein und weiß
das Haus, und der grüne Schimmer,
ein Weidenblatt.

Wind. Er hat mich geführt.
Vor der Schwelle lag ich.
Er hat mich bedeckt. Wohin
sollt ich ihm folgen? Ich hab
Flügel nicht. Meine Mütze
abends
warf ich den Vögeln zu.

Dämmrung. Die Fledermäuse
fahren ums Haupt mir. Das Ruder
zerbrochen, so werd ich nicht sinken, ich gehe
über den Strom.

The Road Home

Blue.
The breezes.
The tall tree
around which the heron flies.
And that house of old
toward which the forest
now descends,
small and white, that house
with its shimmer of green
willow leaf.

Wind. Which guided me.
I lay at the threshold. Wind
which covered me. Where
should I follow it? I have
no wings. Evenings,
I'd toss my cap
to the birds.

Twilight. Bats flit
about my head. The oar
is broken, but I shall not sink, I shall make it
over the river.

(May 18, 1960)

Immer zu benennen

Immer zu benennen:
den Baum, den Vogel im Flug,
den rötlichen Fels, wo der Strom
zieht, grün, und den Fisch
im weißen Rauch, wenn es dunkelt
über die Wälder herab.

Zeichen, Farben, es ist
ein Spiel, ich bin bedenklich,
es möchte nicht enden
gerecht.

Und wer lehrt mich,
was ich vergaß: der Steine
Schlaf, den Schlaf
der Vögel im Flug, der Bäume
Schlaf, im Dunkel
geht ihre Rede—?

Wär da ein Gott
und im Fleisch,
und könnte mich rufen, ich würd
umhergehn, ich würd
warten ein wenig.

Always to Be Named

Always to be named:
the tree, the bird in flight,
the reddish rock, where the river
flows, green, and the fish
in the white mist, when the dark
descends upon the woods.

Signs, colors, it is
a game. Which, it occurs to me,
might not do it justice.

And who shall teach me
what I've forgotten: the sleep
of stones, the sleep
of birds in flight, the sleep
of trees, does their speech
move in the dark?

Were there a God,
and in the flesh,
and were he to call out to me, I might
wander about, I might
wait a bit more.

(February 4, 1961)

Mickiewicz

Vor dem Eichenwald bin ich, das Schloß
stumm, eine Kerze
stellte die Mutter
unter das Bild im Wilnaer Tor, auf dem Strom
flogen Segel, im Rauch,
der Habicht fuhr
über die Bläue, ein roter
Abend ist ihm gefolgt

und eine Zeit der Städte
und eine der Straßen, der Felssturz
Krim, vor dem Meer
Wegstaub erhob sich, der Wagen
kam durch die Steppe von Akkerman—

Ich gewöhn mich ins Glück,
ich sage, es ist ganz leicht,
ich denk, meine Stimme trägt,
ich trink einen Regen, zurück
leg ich den Kopf auf die Mauer
Paris, ich trinke den Himmel
wie einen Mund, ich seh,
den die Lüfte erheben, den Habicht
über dem Eichwald, der Strom
führt einen Bogen hinab
in die Ebenen, fort,
unter den Schwalbenlüften
fort, aus der rieselnden Frühe,
über die Dörfer gespannt
und die Wälder: der Tag,
glänzend vom Zorn, einer Rüstung—

Mickiewicz

I come from the oak woods, the castle
fallen silent, a candle
placed by my mother
beneath the icon at the Vilna gate, sails
winging downstream in the mist,
the hawk soaring
over the blue, followed
by the blush of dusk

and a time for cities,
a time for streets, and the rockslides
of Crimea, and the dust kicked up
on roads by the sea, and the coach
making its way across the steppes from Akkerman—

I get used to happiness,
I say it's a lark,
I imagine my voice carries,
I drink of the rain, I lean
my head against the Paris
walls, I gulp up the skies
like a mouth, I see,
aloft in the winds, the hawk
over the oak wood, the river
as it loops through the plains,
and then day
breaking forth
from the swallow breezes
as it tightens its light over village
and wood—day, its coat of mail
ablaze with wrath.

Ich werd kommen, vom Singsang
müd, vom Gered, nur den Flug
einer Etüde über dem Ohr, ich werd stehn
auf den Hängen, hören
nach einem Ruf und den Ton
suchen mit zitterndem Mund,
sagen: es ist ganz leicht.

I shall come, tired of all this singsong,
tired of all this talk, with the sole flight
of an étude over my ear, I shall stand
on the cliffs, I shall listen
for a call, I shall search out the note
with my pursed lips, and say:
It's a lark.

(May 7, 1961)

FROM

Weathersigns (1966)

Wetterzeichen

J. S. Bach

Unbequemer Mann,
Stadtpfeifergemüt, mit Degen
wie mit Neigung zum Sentiment
(praktikabel, versteht sich),
einer Kinderfreude
an plätschernden Wassern, stetig
wirkendem Gang der Flüsse;
so sind der kahle Jordan
und der von Himmeln trächtige
Euphrat ihm
freundlich.

Daß er die Meerbucht sah—
einen dort, der herging
hinter Feuern unsichtbar,
der die Planeten rief
mit einer alten Qual,—

manchmal
im blitzenden Köthener Spiel,
im Bürgerprunk
der Leipziger Jahre
taucht das herauf. Zum Ende
hat er des Pfingstgeists Sausen
nicht mehr gehört mit Trompete
oder Posaune (auf 16 Fuß).

Flöten gehn ihm voraus,
als er müdegeschrieben
tritt vor sein altertümliches Haus,

J. S. Bach

An awkward presence,
court trumpeter by birth, sword at thigh,
yet inclined to sentiment
(should the occasion arise),
a child's delight in the plash
of fountains or the decisive
rush of rivers, so that
both Jordan's bleak stream
and the fertile skies
of the Euphrates
prove congenial to him.

That he saw the bay—
someone there, making his way,
invisible, behind the fires,
calling out to the planets
in his torment of old—

at times
in those flashing performances at Köthen
or in the bourgeois pomp
of his Leipzig years
this emerges. In the end
he could no longer hear
the spirit of Pentecost swoop down
in trumpet or trombone (at 16').

Flutes precede him
when dead-tired from composing
he steps out of his ancient house,

den fliegenden Wind
spürt, die Erde
nicht mehr erkennt.

sensing the racing wind,
but no longer recognizes
the earth.

(June 25, 1958)

Hechtzeit

Wurzeln,
haltet mich,
Eschenwurzeln,
ich fall aus dem Erdreich, geäderter
Stein, den ein Schwalbenflügel
streifte! Weißbrust, Schwalbe,
flieg auf dem Nebelpfad.

Den bitteren Hecht
riß ich vom Grunde los,
schlug ihn gegen den Stein,
eh sein Grün verblaßte,
um das Blut
bog ich Blätter vom Klettenstrauch.

Kahn,
bring mich hinüber.
Weiß ist der Himmel. Ein Baum
aus Vogelrufen
schlägt seine Augen auf.

Pike Time

Roots,
take hold of me,
ash-tree roots,
I'm falling out of the world, veined
stone, grazed by swallow
wing. White-chested martin,
fly the path of mist.

I tore the bitter pike loose
from the streambed
and slapped it against a stone,
before it went pale green
I wrapped burdock leaves
around its blood.

Skiff,
ferry me across.
The sky's white. A tree
of birdcalls
opens its eyes.

(1960)

Auf einen Brunnen

Vergeßlich sein—
Brunnen.
Hinter den Erlen
der Wiesenrauch. Du wirst
schöpfen den Sand, das Wasser
fällt.

Auf die Reuse der Wälder
erhob sich der Strom.
Über die Quellen warf er
Strauchwerk und Schilf. Der Schwarzbart
hob die Hand aus dem Kaftan.
Die Flößer zogen voraus.

Brunnen, dein Moos ist verdorrt.
Balkengeviert, du sankst
über den Sand. Zerbrich,
Brunnenbaum, über die Stimme
unter dem Sand, die Stimme
breite dich, Baum, aus vier Winden,
Rose, siebenblättrig,
steh in den Lüften—dort
weh auch der Schnee.

To a Fountain

To forget it all—
fountain.
Behind the alders,
the meadow scent. You shall
bring forth sand, the water level
sinks.

Among the fish weirs of the woods
the river was born,
clogging the springs
with shrubs and reeds. Blackbeard
raised his hand from his caftan.
Raftsmen poled downstream.

Fountain, your moss in disarray,
you sank in tatters
among the sands. Fountain
tree, break free
from the murmuring bank, tree,
let your voice widen with the four winds.
Rose, let your seven petals
rise into the breeze, among
the blowing snows.

(May 13, 1961)

Der Freund

Ein Trinklied das nicht gesungen wird
nur gehört
zum Getön der Zikade
einem Gesträuch wo die Bläue hinabreicht
bis an die Erde

Ölbaum Abend hinaus
gehen die Schatten
für ein Gespräch mit Lampen und Lichtern der Greis
tritt aus der Schenke
vor zweitausend Jahren Kavafis

Der dich nicht sah die Hand überm Blick
mit zuckender Schulter die Strophe
hörte er dich
schwarz die Schale attisch
mit des Euphronios roter Figur

The Friend

A drinking song not on the lips
barely audible
in the cicada's chirr
a bouquet whose blue skies
reach down to the earth

On olive tree evenings
the shades emerge
to fall into talk with the lights and lamps
as the old man takes his leave from Cavafy's
two-thousand-year-old café

Who never saw you shield your eyes
with your hand as you shrugged your shoulders
now heard your strophe
the black of the Attic vase
the Euphronios figure in red

(June 28, 1961)

Mozart

Am Schuh die Schnalle
ist lose, ein silberner Knopf
hat hier gesessen, mich schmerzt
der Hals, die Augen,
wenn ich sie schlösse—

Damals fiel mir auf
die neue Falte
in Colloredos Gesicht—
in Prag das Häuschen,
schwimmend über den Hang,
Gesträuch, eine weiße Woge,
vor sich her—als der endlose
Regen vorüber war, eines
Abends das Licht
auf dem Stainschen Clavier.

Es gab noch zu schreiben
eine Musik,
Holz, ein Dröhnen, irdisch,
unter den Füßen, im Haus
schlägt eine Tür, ich frag nicht,
ich hör sie allein,
ich hab es nicht gern, wenn Constanze
mit dem gläsernen Munde
lacht.

Mozart

My shoe buckle
is loose, a silver button
used to sit there, my throat
and eyes sore
when I close them—

Back then I was struck
by the fresh crease
on Colloredo's face,
by the tiny house in Prague
perched on the cliff,
bushes, a white wave
receding, as the endless rain
at last let up and
the evening light
fell on the Stain pianoforte.

There was still music
left to write, wood-
winds, a deep earthy drone
underfoot, a door banging
in the house, I ask no questions,
I alone hear the music,
I can't stand it when Constanze
opens her glass mouth
to laugh.

(July 9, 1961)

Im Strom

Mit den Flößen hinab
im helleren Grau des fremden
Ufers, einem
Glanz, der zurücktritt, dem Grau
schräger Flächen, aus Spiegeln
beschoß uns das Licht.

Es lag des Täufers Haupt
auf der zerrissenen Schläfe,
in das verschnittene Haar
eine Hand mit bläulichen, losen
Nägeln gekrallt.

Als ich dich liebte, unruhig
dein Herz, die Speise auf schlagendem
Feuer, der Mund, der sich öffnete,
offen, der Strom
war ein Regen und flog
mit den Reihern, Blätter
fielen und füllten sein Bett.

Wir beugten uns über erstarrte
Fische, mit Schuppen bekleidet
trat der Grille Gesang
über den Sand, aus den Lauben
des Ufers, wir waren gekommen
einzuschlafen, Niemand
umschritt das Lager, Niemand
löschte die Spiegel, Niemand

Midstream

Drifting down on rafts
into the brighter gray of the foreign
shore, a sudden
gleam, retreating onto the gray
slant of the rocks, mirrored
light shot down on us.

There lay the Baptist's head,
at its fractured skull,
at its ragged hair
clawed a hand
with loose bluish nails.

When I loved you, your heart
was restless, the pot on the roaring
fire, your mouth, when opened,
open wide, the river turning
into rain and fleeing away
with the herons, the leaves
falling and filling its bed.

As we bent over the stiff dead
fish, the call of the cricket, clad
in scales, rang out
over the sands, we had left
the leafy woods to come sleep here
by the shore, No One
circled our camp, No One
extinguished the mirrors, No One

wird uns wecken
zu unserer Zeit.

shall wake us
in our times.

(August 11, 1961)

Mitternachtsdorf

Im verwinkelten Himmel
mit schwerem Fuß
tappt durch den Schatten Saturn
und pfeift seinen Monden.

Aus dem zerbrochnen Dach
wär es zu sehen, aber
das Haus ganz voll von Schlaf
wie von Wäldern
rührt sich im Schlaf,
auf seinem Atem mit offenen
Flügeln schlafen die Vogel.

Laß uns schlafen einer
des andern Schlaf und hören
nicht die Sterne und alle
Stimmen im Finstren, das Blut
nur wie es fällt und zurücksinkt
mit rotgeränderten, schwärzlichen
Blättern unter das Herz.

Morgen magst du verstreun
Asche über den Himmel,
vor die näherkommenden
Schritte Saturns.

Midnight Village

Across the angled sky
Saturn plods
through the shadows,
whistling to his moons.

Which could have been glimpsed
through the broken roof, but
the house was too busy sleeping,
though now and then it stirred
like a forest, the birds
asleep on its breath
with open wings.

Let's sleep each other's
sleep, let's not listen
to all the stars or voices
in the dark, but only to the pulse
of blood, as its red-edged, blackish
leaves now lift and fall back
upon the heart.

Tomorrow, go strew
ashes over the sky
as Saturn's steps
grow near.

(August 19, 1961)

Der lettische Herbst

Das Tollkirschendickicht
ist geöffnet, er tritt
auf die Lichtung, vergessen wird
um die Birkenstümpfe der Hühnertanz, er geht
vorüber am Baum, den die Reiher umflogen, auf Wiesen,
er hat gesungen.

Ach daß der Schwaden Heu,
wo er lag in der hellen Nacht,
das Heu zerstreut mit den Winden
flög auf den Ufern—

wenn nicht mehr wach ist der Strom,
die Wolke über ihm, Stimme
der Vögel, Rufe:
Wir kommen nicht mehr—

Dann entzünd ich dein Licht,
das ich nicht sehn kann, die Hände
legt' ich darüber, dicht
um die Flamme, sie blieb
stehen rötlich vor lauter Nacht
(wie die Burg, die herabkam
über den Hang zerfallen,
wie mit Flügeln das Schlänglein
Licht durch den Strom, wie das Haar
des Judenkindes)
und brannte mich nicht.

Latvian Autumn

The thicket of deadly nightshade
now thrown open, he steps
into the clearing, the dance of hens
around birch stumps now forgotten, makes his way
past the tree round which the herons flew, having sung
in the meadows.

Ah, that the bed of hay
on which he lay in the bright of night
might now take wing, scattered
shoreward by the winds—

when the river is no longer awake,
in the clouds above the voices
of birds call out:
We shall come no more—

Then I light your light
which I cannot see, I placed
my hands over it, close to
the flame, which blazed red
the whole night through
(like that castle on fire
upon the cliff, like that feather of light
that snaked through the stream,
like the red hair
of that Jewish child)
yet did not burn me.

(October 10, 1961)

Schattenland

Die Raschelstimmen,
Blätter, Vögel, drei Wege
kam ich
vor einem großen Schnee.
Auf dem Ufer, Grannen und Kletten
im Ringelhaar, mit ihren Hunden
Ragana schrie nach dem Fährmann, im Wasser
stand er, mitten im Fluß.

Einmal
folgend den Nebeln,
über die Senke mit goldenen Flügeln
zogen die Trappen, sie setzten
auf die Gräser den hornigen Fuß,
Licht flog, der Tag ihnen nach.

Kalt. Auf der Spitze des Grashalms
die Leere weiß
bis an den Himmel. Der Baum
aber alt, dort ist
ein Ufer, Nebel mit dünnen
Gelenken gehn auf dem Fluß.

Finsternis, wer hier lebt,
spricht mit des Vogels Stimme.
Ausgefahren sind
Windlichter über den Wäldern.
Kein Atem hat sie bewegt.

Shadowland

The rustle of voices,
leaves, birds, by three roads
I came upon
deep snow.
On the shore, all burls and bristles
and ringlets of hair, with her dogs
Ragana shouted to the ferryman, out there
on the water, midstream.

Time was,
following the fogs
over the hollows with their golden wings,
the bustards set
their bony feet upon the grass,
pursued by day.

Cold. At the tip of the grass blade,
emptiness, white
as far as the sky. But an old tree
there, the shore
there, slim limbs of mist
astride the river.

Darkness, whoever lives here
speaks with the voice of a bird.
Over the woods the lanterns
have drifted off, driven
by no breath of air.

(January 20, 1962)

An Klopstock

Wenn ich das Wirkliche nicht
wollte, dieses: ich sag
Strom und Wald,
ich hab in die Sinne aber
gebunden die Finsternis,
Stimme des eilenden Vogels, den Pfeilstoß
Licht um den Abhang

und die tönenden Wasser—
wie wollt ich
sagen deinen Namen,
wenn mich ein kleiner Ruhm
fände—ich hab
aufgehoben, dran ich vorüberging,
Schattenfabel von den Verschuldungen
und der Sühnung:
so als den Taten
trau ich—du führtest sie—trau ich
der Vergeßlichen Sprache,
sag ich hinab in die Winter
ungeflügelt, aus Röhricht
ihr Wort.

To Klopstock

Were I not to want
the real, as is: I'd say
river and wood, but
having bound the dark
into my senses, the voice
of the hurried bird, the light
arrowing over the slope

and the rush of the waters—
how speak your name
if visited by minor
fame—I've preserved
what I've passed through,
a shadow tale of guilt
and atonement:
just as I trust in acts
(following you), I trust
the language of those who forget,
deep into the winters,
unwinged, I speak
their word
of reed.

(February 5, 1962)

Erfahrung

Zeichen,
Kreuz und Fisch,
an die Steinwand geschrieben der Höhle.

Die Prozession der Männer
taucht hinab in die Erde.
Der Boden wölbt sich herauf,
Kraut, grünlich, gewachsen
durch ein Gesträuch.

Gegen die Brust
steht mir der Strom auf,
die Stimme aus Sand:

öffne dich
ich kann nicht hindurch
deine toten
treiben in mir

Experience

Signs,
cross and fish,
written on the rock cave wall.

The procession of men
descends into the earth.
The ground arches up,
weeds, greenish, push
through the shrubs.

The river rises
against my breast,
the voice of sand:

Open up,
I can't make it through,
all your dead so
unruly in me.

(February 16, 1962)

Begegnung

Vom überhängenden Baum
mit Namen
rief ich den wütenden Fisch.
Ich schrieb um den weißen Mond
eine Figur, geflügelt.
Aufträumt ich des Jägers Traum,
er beschlafe ein Wild.

Gewölk zieht über dem Strom,
das ist meine Stimme,
Schneelicht über den Wäldern,
das ist mein Haar.
Über den finsteren Himmel
kam ich des Wegs,
Gras im Mund, mein Schatten
lehnte am Holzzaun, er sagte:
Nimm mich zurück.

Encounter

From the overhanging tree
I called the angry fish
by name.
Around the white moon
I traced a figure, wingèd.
I dreamt the hunter's dream
of sleeping with his prey.

Clouds scud over the river,
this is my voice,
snow light over woods,
this is my hair.
Across the darkening sky
I made my way,
grass in my mouth, my shadow
on the fence, saying:
Take me back.

(March 18, 1962)

Wiesenfluß

Kalt ist der Sommer, Licht
fährt mit Segeln, der Fisch
mit den Flossen
steht auf der Schattenspur.

Ich bin gewachsen zu hören
die Quelle im Kalmusherzen,
weiß und rötlich, die Dehnung,
ich komm, und der Wasserläufer
unterbricht sich, der Fisch
stürzt mit dem eigenen Glanz
über die Tiefe.

Hör, hier bin ich, ich geh
umher
in der Kälte des Sommers.

Meadowbrook

The summer is cold, the light
luffs like a sail, and the fish
tracks down shadows
with its fins.

I have grown to hear
the wellspring of the calamus,
white, reddish, extending,
here I come, and the water skipper
breaks its stride, and the fish,
aglint, dives
over the deep.

Listen, here I am, coursing
this way and that
in the chill of summer.

(April 22, 1962)

Herberge

Licht, herab
mit des Klettenblatts
Neigung, die Zeile Licht—
Wind, der gläserne Flügel
rührt auf dem Ufer.

Komm und geh und kehr wieder,
komm und bleib, ein Haus,
Nebelhaus, steht vor dem Wald,
Dächer aus Rauch,
Türme aus Vogelrufen,
Birkenzweige abends verschließen die Tür.

Ruhlos liegen wir dort,
Schattentuch auf der Schulter,
um die Fischerfeuer
gehn mit den rötlichen Flossen
die Lüfte, du sprichst, fremde Stimme,
ich hör dich mit fremdem Ohr.

Sanctuary

Light, falling
with the cling of burdock
burr, a strip of light—
wind, its glass wing
grazing the shore.

Come and go and return once more,
come and stay, a house,
a house of mist, at forest's edge,
roofs of smoke,
towers of birdcalls,
birch branches barring the gates at dusk.

There we lie and get no rest,
shadow shawls upon our shoulders,
the red fins of the winds
flit about the fishermen's lights,
you speak, O foreign voice—
with a foreign ear I hear you.

(May 23, 1962)

Die Wolgastädte

Der Mauerstrich.
Türme. Die Stufe des Ufers. Einst,
die hölzerne Brücke zerriß. Über die Weite fuhren
Tatarenfeuer. Mit strähnigem Bart
Nacht, ein Wandermönch, kam
redend. Die Morgen
schossen herauf, die Zisternen
standen im Blut.

Geh umher auf dem Stein.
Hier im gläsernen Mittag
über die Augen hob
Minin die Hand. Dann Geschrei
stob herauf, den Wassern entgegen, Stjenkas
Ankunft—Es gehn auf dem Ufer
bis an die Hüften im Unterholz
Sibiriaken, ihre
Wälder ziehn ihnen nach.

Dort
einen Menschenmund
hörte ich rufen:
Komm in dein Haus
durch die vermauerte Tür,
die Fenster schlag auf
gegen das Lichtmeer.

Volga Towns

The stretch of wall.
Towers. The riverbank's slope. Back when
the wooden bridge broke apart. Tartar fires
advanced across the plain. Scraggly-bearded
Night, a wandering monk, turned up
with things to say. The mornings
shot upward, the cisterns
aswim with blood.

Pick your way among the stones.
Here against the glassy midday sun
Minin raised his hand
to shield his eyes. Then a great shout
went out over the waters to greet Stenka's
arrival, with the Siberians crawling up
the bank, up to their waists
in the underbrush, forests
in their wake.

There
I heard a human mouth call out:
Come into your house
through the bricked-up door.
Fling every window open
to the sea of light.

(June 2, 1962)

Mit deiner Stimme

Mit deiner Stimme
bis in die Nacht
redet der Weidenbusch, Lichter
fliegen um ihn.
Hoch, eine Wasserblume
fährt durch die Finsternis.
Mit seinen Tieren
atmet der Fluß.

In den Kalmus
trage ich mein geflochtenes Haus.
Die Schnecke
unhörbar
geht über mein Dach.
Eingezeichnet
in meine Handflächen
finde ich dein Gesicht.

With your voice

With your voice
far into the night
the dappled willow speaks, the lights
swirl around it.
On high, a water-blossom
drifts through the dark.
With every creature
the river breathes.

Into the calamus
I carry my wattled house.
The snake slithers
soundless
over my roof.
Marked
on my palms
I find your face.

(June 20, 1962)

Das Ende der Sommernacht

Der Distelkopf
schlägt nach den Lichtern
über dem Wasser. Ein Vogel
hat Zeichen geschrieben
ins Eschenlaub. Um die Wurzeln
von Schilf und Rohr
legt aus der Fisch sein Flossenrot.

Aufgestanden ist
gegen den Ruhm
der Staub.
Er, aus den Säulen der Nebel,
tritt in die Ebenen, über
die Flüsse, dunkel
rührt er die Feuer an.

Summer Night's End

The thistle head
strikes at the lights
over the water. A bird
has scratched signs
upon the ash leaves. The fish flashes
the reds of its fins
around the roots of rush and reed.

Dust
has risen up
against fame.
Out of the pillars of mist
it moves into the plains, across
rivers, and, dark,
touches on their fires.

(July 1962)

Kalmus

Mit Regensegeln umher
fliegt, ein Geheul,
der Wasserwind.
Eine blaue Taube
hat die Flügel gebreitet
über den Wald.
Schön im zerbrochenen Eisen
der Farne
geht das Licht
mit dem Kopf eines Fasans.

Atem,
ich sende dich aus,
find dir ein Dach,
geh ein durch ein Fenster, im weißen
Spiegel erblick dich,
dreh dich lautlos,
ein grünes Schwert.

Calamus

Under sails of rain
the water-wind flees
in howls.
A blue dove
has spread its wings
over the woods.
In the broken armor
of the ferns
the pheasant-headed light
now stirs.

Breath,
I send you forth,
go find yourself a roof,
go enter a window, look
at yourself in the white of the mirror,
twirl about without a sound,
green sword.

(August 20, 1962)

Die Ostseestädte

Das Licht ohne Aufgang und Niedergang.
Das Wasser, das sich am Tod der Falter belebt.
Regen ist Regen.
Der Wind, der unter der Wolke
in Hadern daherkommt,
hat den Sand der Flüsse gestrählt, eine Düne
geführt über die See.

Licht
kommt zurück
über das Wasser. Regen
findet den Weg
den Vögeln nach. Bunte Tafeln
sind aufgeschlagen
in den zerbröckelnden hohen
Gemäuern landauf, landab.
Dort steht zu lesen:
Es wuchs das Gras.

Baltic Sea Towns

The light without rise or fall.
The waters revived by drowned butterflies.
Rain is rain.
The wind that comes in squalls
beneath the clouds
has furrowed the river's sands
and led a dune to sea.

Light
returns
over the waters. Rain discovers
the paths
birds take. Painted panels
unfold on high crumbling
altar walls
up and down the land.
On which one reads:
Here lay the grass.

(September 4, 1962)

Das Wasser

Du sprichst noch,
Wasser, du sprichst,
du kamst im Gesträuch mit den kleinen
Schritten unter dem Wind;
er suchte die Flüsse hinter
der Finsternis und das Boot,
darin der Mond fährt, im Heu,
du hörtest ihn sagen:
Hier sind die Weiden,
hier ist das Eulenhaus.

Aber der Mond blickt hinaus auf die Feuer am Sinai.
Aber das Wasser hört die Fröste von Skythien her.
Aber die Vogelschwärme heben sich über die Wälder.
Aber der Schnee vor dem Himmel errichtet sein Dach.

Water

You go on speaking
and speaking, water,
and step by tiny step you entered
the bushes beneath the wind
that sought out the rivers behind
the dark and the boat
on which the moon sails in the hay,
and you heard it speak:
Here are the willows,
here is the house of the owl.

But the moon gazes upon the fires of Sinai.
But the water hears the coming of the Scythian frosts.
But the bird flocks fly over the woods.
But the snow raises its roof against the skies.

(September 12, 1962)

An Runge

Rückwege: hinter
Wolgast die Straße
auf weißen Schuhn, die Feuer
sommers, die grünen
Lichter, der Sund
unter dem Bogen, der hing
an Ketten, der Tag,
und ging auf dem Wasser.

Runge, der Blick
über die Schulter, der Schritt
aus der Tür, eine Münze
unter der Zunge, ein kleines
Silber—hinter den Zäunen
Schatten,
über die Wiesen mit hohem Haupt
kommt der Feldberg und redet
in Vogelsprüchen.

To Runge

Ways homeward: behind
Wolgast, on the road
in white shoes, the fires
of summer, the green
lights, the bay
beneath the rainbow, hung there
on a chain, day making
its way upon the waters.

Runge, the glance
over your shoulder, the step
out of your door, a coin
under your tongue, a bit
of silver—behind the shadows
of the fences,
over the meadows, head held high,
the Feldberg arrives, speaking
in bird rhymes.

(October 11, 1962)

Sprache

Der Baum
größer als die Nacht
mit dem Atem der Talseen
mit dem Geflüster über
der Stille

Die Steine
unter dem Fuß
die leuchtenden Adern
lange im Staub
für ewig

Sprache
abgehetzt
mit dem müden Mund
auf dem endlosen Weg
zum Hause des Nachbarn

Language

The tree
taller than night
with its lake breath
with its whisper
through stillness

The stones
underfoot
veins aglow
in the everlasting
dust

Speech
harried
mouth worn out
on the endless path
to the neighbor's house

(February 26, 1963)

Wenn verlassen sind

Wenn verlassen sind
die Räume, in denen Antworten erfolgen, wenn
die Wände stürzen und Hohlwege, aus den Bäumen
fliegen die Schatten, wenn aufgegeben ist
unter den Füßen das Gras,
weiße Sohlen betreten den Wind—

der Dornbusch flammt,
ich hör seine Stimme,
wo keine Frage war, ein Gewässer
geht, doch mich dürstet nicht.

When they have been deserted

When they have been deserted,
these rooms that give rise to answers, when
the walls and corridors crumble, shadows flee
the trees, when the grass
underfoot is abandoned,
white soles tread the wind—

the thornbush bursts into flame,
I hear its voice,
where there was no question, the water
flows, yet I do not thirst.

(April 15, 1963)

Vogelnest

Mein Himmel
wechselt mit deinem,
auch meine Taube
jetzt
überfliegt die deine,
ich seh zwei Schatten
fallen
im Haferfeld.

Wir vertauschen
unsere Augen,
wir finden
ein Lager:
Regen,
wir sagen
wie eine Geschichte
die halben Sätze
Grün,
ich hör:

Zu meiner Braue
hinauf
mit Vogelreden
dein Mund
trägt Federn und Zweige.

Bird Nest

My sky
changes with yours,
even as my dove
now over-
flies yours,
I see two shadows
converge
in the oat field.

We trade
eyes,
we pitch
camp:
rain,
like a tale
we tell
half sentences
of green,
I hear:

Approaching my brow
with birdcall
your mouth
bears
feathers and twigs.

(May 2, 1963)

Jakub Bart in Ralbitz

Eulenschreie—
so in der Nacht
reden die Dörfer, wie sag ich,
daß ihr mich hört,
Sorben, es kommen die Fremden,
sie sagen:
ihr seid Tote, ihr seid
wenige, lernt zu schweigen,
streckt euch ins Grab.

Wacht doch,
daß ihr vernehmt
die Brüder hinter der Grenze,
über den Bergen wie Feuer,
über den Wäldern, es gehn
die Stürme
brüderlich, ihr hört:
sie reden mit eueren Mündern,
sie treten wie ihr die Erde,
sie gehn aus den Gruben
herauf wie ihr.

Aber wer,
daß ich rede,
bin ich geworden?
"Wehe, Stern, du bist
gefallen in Finsternis,
in das Getöse
aus blauer Höhe, der Höhe
ohne Laut"—
dorthinauf

Jakub Bart in Ralbitz

Owl cries—
thus the villages speak
at night, how say this
so that you might hear me,
Sorbs, the foreigners are on their way,
claiming:
You are the dead, you are
the few, learn to shut your mouths,
lie down in your graves.

But awake,
that you might lay eyes
upon your brothers beyond the border,
over the hills, like fire,
over the forests, the storms
make their fraternal way
into your ear:
they talk with your mouths,
they walk the earth as you do,
like you they ascend
from the mine pits.

But who
am I now one
to speak?
"Woe to you, star,
fallen into darkness,
into chaos,
out of the blue, from the heights
of silence"—
to which

erheb ich mich, es erhebt mich,
das seine Stimme gewann,
mein Volk.

I aspire, overjoyed
my people
has won its speech.

(May 8, 1963)

Ankunft

1.
Meine Tür
hat dich gerufen, ich schloß
das Fenster, verhängt' die zerbrochene
Scheibe, die Wolke,
ein Dach unter fallenden Lüften,
hob sich, es durchblühten
Malven das Stroh, aus dem Regen
nahm ich das Licht, aus schlagendem
Wasser das Licht, so verbrannt ich
das Dunkel im Haus.

Unter der Tür,
die Wange
fragte den Mund, die Schulter
gab der Hüfte zur Antwort:
Damals entflogst du, Herbst
war noch sichtbar, Winter
fuhr mit den Lichtern, roten
Feuern, du lebtest von Fremdem.
Grün, ein Riß zog im Eis.
Stöhnen war auf dem Strom.
Weiß auf dem Schnee.

Arrival

1.
My door
called out to you, I shut
the window, covered the broken
pane, the cloud,
a roof against the sinking breezes,
was pitched, the mallows bloomed
through the straw, from the rain
I gathered the light, the light
of the downpour, thus burning off
the darkness from the house.

Under the door,
the cheek whispered to
the mouth, the shoulder
answered to the hip:
Back when you flew off, autumn
was still visible, winter coming in,
all lights and reddish
fires, you lived off strangers.
Green, a crack in the ice.
A groan upon the river.
A whitening of snow.

(August 2, 1961)

2.
Der auf dich zutritt, ich,
sagt nicht: Sieh mich kommen.

Weiß auf dem Weg
gingst du, die weißen Rufe
flogen der Dörfer, die grüne
Stimme des Ufers,
es wuchsen herauf
Himbeerzweige durch unsere
Hände. Weiß und Grün.

Wer denn steht
hinter den Türen, lauscht:
Ein Klopfen
geht unterm Dach?

Hier wird sprechen,
der vor das Tor tritt, der
Lebendige, er wird sagen:

Wer des Wegs kommt,
trete herein.

2.

This I, who approached you,
does not say: See me coming.

White on your way
you went, white cries
flew from the villages, green
voices of the shore,
raspberry branches
rising through
our hands. White and green.

Who lurks
behind doors, listening:
A knock
in the attic?

Here shall speak
who is stationed at the gate,
alive enough to say:

Wayfarer,
welcome in.

(June 17, 1963)

Antwort

Über dem Zaun
deine Rede:
Von den Bäumen fällt die Last,
der Schnee.

Auch im gestürzten Holunder
das Schwirrlied der Amseln, der Grille
Gräserstimme
kerbt Risse ins Mauerwerk, Schwalbenflug
steil
gegen den Regen, Sternbilder
gehn auf dem Himmel,
im Reif.

Die mich einscharren
unter die Wurzeln,
hören:
er redet,
zum Sand,
der ihm den Mund füllt—so wird
reden der Sand, und wird
schreien der Stein, und wird
fliegen das Wasser.

Answer

From the other side of the fence
you say: See how
the trees unburden themselves
of snow.

Whir of blackbird song
in the toppled elder, crickets'
reedy voices notching
chinks in the brickwork, swallow flights
steep
into the rain, constellations
glide across the sky
in the hoarfrost.

Let those who would bury me
beneath the roots
hear:
he addresses
all the sand crammed
down his throat—that
the sand might speak, that
the stone cry out, that
water take wing.

(July 17, 1963)

Nachtfischer

Im schönen Laub
die Stille
unverschmerzt.
Licht
mit den Händen
über einer Mauer.
Der Sand tritt aus den Wurzeln.
Sand, geh rot
im Wasser fort,
geh auf der Spur der Stimmen,
im Finstern geh,
leg aus den Fang am Morgen.
Die Stimmen singen silberblaß,
bring fort,
in Sicherheit,
ins schöne Laub die Ohren,
die Stimmen singen:
tot ist tot

Night Fisher

Among these lovely leaves
the silence
unblemished.
Light
by handfuls
over a wall.
Sand spills from the roots.
Sand, go red
in the water,
go track the trail of voices,
go into the dark,
display your catch at dawn.
The voices sing silver-pale,
let your ears
escape to safety
in these lovely leaves,
the voices singing:
Dead is dead.

(July 19, 1963)

Barlach in Güstrow

Steine,
den vielfachen Bogen
verschließt
mit Eisenadern
die Tür. An der Schwelle
die Erde
mit wenig Gras und Wegerich.
Ich steh,
den Stock an mich gezogen.

Das ist nichts:
umhergehn, andere Wege.
Wer das war,
der ins verschlossene Grün
tönerne Vögel setzte,
hab ich vergessen.
Er saß an der Weide. Mit Rauchfahnen
ungesichtig
geht dieser Tag.

Rauch.
Dort der Bogen.
Licht stürzt die Dächer herab.
Der Kiesel unter dem Schuh,
abends, der Kiesel,
abends
der Kiesel
gefangen.

Barlach in Güstrow

Stones,
the various arches
barred
by the door's
iron veins. At its sill,
a world
with little grass or plantain.
I stand,
clutching my walking stick.

No matter:
to wander about, find other ways.
Who it was
who set these birds of sculpted clay
into this enclosed garden
I now forget.
He sat by the pasture. With wisps
of smoke, day feels
its blind way.

Smoke.
Over there, the rainbow.
Light streams down the roofs.
The pebbles underfoot
at nightfall, pebble
after pebble
caught
in the dark.

(August 7, 1963)

Strandgänger

Noch immer
über dem Schilfland
die Mittagsflamme, über
der Düne
noch immer nicht
das Rauschen der Schwäne, noch immer
das Salzkraut
lautlos,
die Hände im Sand.

Wenn das Sternzeichen fliegt
über dem Sund,
Eis an den Flügeln,
die Wälder aus Grillenstimmen
heraufgehn
über die Öde,
mit hohlen Mündern reden
hinab auf die See—

ich hör dich kommen, du trittst
aus deinen Schatten, wirfst
von der Schulter die Last
Schwemmholz, aus der Hand
huscht dir ein Feuer.

Dich werd ich fragen:
Wie heiß ich?
Wo bin ich?
Wie lang noch
bleibe ich hier?

Beachcomber

Midday still
aflame
over the expanse of weeds, over
the dunes
still
no whir of swan flight,
the saltwort still
silent,
hands in the sand.

When the constellation glides
over the straits,
ice at its wings,
forests of cricket calls
rise up
over the wastes
to speak, hollow-mouthed,
to the sea below—

I hear you coming, you step
from your shadow and cast
your load of driftwood
from your shoulders, a spark
flitting from your hand.

To you I'll ask:
What's my name?
Where am I?
How long will I
here remain?

(August 7, 1963)

J. M. R. Lenz

"Schnurrpfeifer,
da red her!"

Das ist der niedliche Lenz.
Geht durchs Gebirg.
Liegt auf einer Straße
im zeitigen Frühjahr,
da verläuft sich das Wasser
in Moskau 1792,
da spitzt er nicht mehr
den Mund.

War einiges zu reden,
erinnere ich mich,
aber das ist geschehen,
denk ich, ich hör,
man hat es
gehört.

Daß die Hauslehrer
ein Pferd brauchen. Die Offiziers
auch irgend so etwas. Daß
der Winterhimmel herabfiel
im Monat Mai,
als jemand weggegangen
war, ich wußte nicht: wohin.

Aber nicht reden
jetzt.
Es dröhnt, zu den Augen herein.
Hinter Riga, der Stadt, ging der Himmel umher.

J. M. R. Lenz

"Whimsical whistler,
natter on!"

Thus the adorable Lenz.
He walks through the mountains.
He lies on a street
in the early spring,
the water flooding
Moscow in 1792,
his mouth no longer
in a pout.

Were there something to say,
I would remember,
but all this did in fact take place,
I think, so I hear,
from what others
have surmised.

That private tutors
need horses. That officers
also need something of the sort. That
the winter sky collapsed
in the month of May
when someone went off,
I know not where.

But say nothing
now.
Threatening weather, deep to the eye.
Behind Riga, an uproar of sky,

Über den Petriturm,
höher noch
sprangen die Wasser.

the waters leaping
over the tower of Saint Peter's
or even higher.

(August 9, 1963)

Namen für den Verfolgten

Der hereinkommt,
im verhängten Fenster
spricht er die Namen nach,
die ich ihm gebe,
Vogelnamen und
den Namen des Raubaals.

gerwe sagt er
wie eine Kranichfeder die Luft streicht,
angurys wie unter der Wasserfläche
ein Schatten sich naht.

Zuletzt gebe ich ihm
den Namen Holunder, den
Namen des Unhörbaren, der
reif geworden ist
und steht voll Blut.

Names for the Persecuted

The one ushered in
behind the curtained windows
repeats the names
I propose to him,
names of birds and
the broadhead eel.

Gerwe, he says
like a crane's feather stroking the breeze,
angurys, like a shadow
rising to the surface of a pond.

Eventually I offer him
the name of the elder tree, *Holunder,*
the name of the unheard, now
ripe, now standing there,
full of blood.

(August 15, 1963)

An Jawlenskij

Wenn das Wasser fällt,
unter den Vogelschreien
wird sichtbar das Land.
Auch die Röte herab
sinkt unter die Flügel.

Ich hab eine Linie gesehen
in meinen eigenen Augen,
die Spur einer Schnecke, den Atem
über dem Schnee,
die weiß gewordene Braue
der Erde, ein Moos.

To Jawlensky

When the water falls
below the cries of birds
the land comes into view.
Even the red sinks
beneath their wings.
I've seen a line
in my own eye,
a snail's track, a breath
upon the snow,
earth's brow
gone white, club moss.

(August 29, 1963)

Am Tage

Der hat sich abgekehrt
der singt mit den Händen
die Lüfte tun sich auf
und antworten
mit Mündern aus Gold

Es ist eine schöne Stille
wir werden hinabgehn
und den Fischern sagen
fahrt aus
wartet nicht auf die Nacht

By Day

He has turned away
who sings with his hands
as the breezes open
to reply
with mouths of gold

The silence is just right
let's go down
and tell the fishermen
be on your way
don't wait up for night

(August 29, 1963)

Der Blitz

Der mich zuwirft
dem Sand
oder allein der Muschel,
dem Baum
oder der Schnecke
am schwingenden Blatt,
ich stürz in die Heuschreckenzüge,
nah vorüber
geh ich dem Vogelflug,

der gibt mir auch
einen Schlaf wie in Feuern,
einen Atem aus Schnee,
der zeigt einen Hohlweg
die Lüfte hinab.

Heiter fahr ich
über den Wäldern, einsilbig.
Ich hör nicht,
der Redende hört nicht.
Reicht mir ein Wasser herauf,
sagt er,
ich brenne.

Lightning

He who throws sand
my way
or a mere mussel
or a tree
or a snail
swung on a leaf
that now plunges me
into a plague of locusts
just above the flight of birds,

also grants me
sleep amid flames,
a breath of snow,
and guides the winds
down ravines.

Through the woods
I make my glad mono-
syllable way. I hear nothing,
the speaker hears nothing.
Hand me up some water,
he says,
I'm on fire.

(September 2, 1963)

Märkisches Museum

Die Bäume treten
aus ihren Wasserschuhen, es wird
hörbar Gelb, eine Sprache der Steine, Sand
geht auf Händen, es dreht sich
die heitere Luft.

Im Laub
hoch, in den Schatten
die Lichter, die kleinen Blitze
im Tierfell, dort erblickt
die Katze mit weißen Augen
das Nachtweib,
es springt durch die Bäume,
es sitzt auf dem trockenen Ästchen
in engen Kleidern, tut
das Haar vors Gesicht.

Brandenburg Museum

The flowers step out
of their water slippers, their yellows
within earshot, a language of stones, the sand
sticks to the hands, the breezes veer
with joy.

High up
in the leaves, lights
in the shadows, small sparks
in animal fur, the tomcat casts
a white eye
on tonight's wife
as she pounces through the trees
pausing on the brittle branches
in her tight clothes, hiding
her face in her hair.

(September 13, 1963)

Eszther

Das ist
mein Volk.
Das sich zerstreut
unter die Völker
und sitzt im Tor.

Auf den Steinen
der Wildgesichtige
richtet sich auf, die Länder
läßt er ruhen, das Gold
geht mit Flammen
über sein Haupt, er hört mich:

Komme ich um,
so komme ich um, ich erschrak,
deine Herrlichkeit mit
Blitzen jagt durch den Himmel,
das springende Blut
der Trompeten
baut mein Haus.

Esther

This is
my people,
scattered among
peoples,
and sits at the gate.

On the stones
the wild-eyed one
rears up, leaving the lands
in peace, his head astream
with flames of gold,
he hears me:

If I perish, so
let me perish, I took fright,
your glory hunts the skies
with lightning,
the leaping blood
of trumpets
builds my house.

(September 26, 1963)

Krypta / Dom zu Brandenburg

Hier
das Gefäß für die Finsternis:
klirrend, die Wände aber
aufgebrochen gegen
die Schatten und weißen Lichter,
dort gehn vorüber
die Bäume
mit kahlem Haupt.

Alt, Finsternis, du
geh nicht unter die Erde,
nicht die Schritte hinunter,
verhalt den Atem, den Schrei:
Wer deckt meine Augen, wer
hebt meine Arme, wer
trägt mir das Haar?

Daß der Abend, sagst du,
nicht käme—er kommt mit dem Rauch
auf dem Wasser, er nennt
vom andern Ufer herüber
seinen Namen ohne Laut—

daß er nicht käme, du schlag
den Stein an den Glockenrand: so
wird erschallen erzen
die Heldin, auf ihrem Ruf
flügellos

Crypt / Brandenburg Cathedral

Here,
the vessel of darkness:
the creak of its walls
broken open against
the white lights and shadows
overhung
by the thinning
crowns of trees.

O darkness, age-old,
do not go under earth
step by step,
spare your breath, your cry:
Who shall shield my eyes, who
shall raise my arm, who
shall bundle my hair?

That the evening, you say,
might not come—yet now comes as smoke
over water, silently
calling its name
from the farther bank—

that it might not come,
go strike the stone
against bell's rim:
that the heroine, the iron one,
echo forth, and the winds

werden die Lüfte
stehn und werden umhergehn
unbeschuht.

be stripped of their wings
and wander about
without shoes.

(October 18, 1963)

Stadt

Sie sehn, die dein Blut
forderten, sie sehen:
die Wunde eitert nicht aus.
Um die scharfen Ränder
legen sich Nebel. Es geht
an die Polonäse
der Lampen kahlhäuptig. Auch kommt
auf der Schnee.

Hier
springen die Steine, gemalte
Wände, die Treppe
bricht, um die Taubenkadaver
—ihre Standarten—
stellen sich die Rattenheere auf.

Hier wird,
sagt man,
grünen ein Baum
und den Himmel halten,
sagt man,
auf Zweigen und Blättern.

City

Those who called for your blood
now see: the wound
has not ceased to fester.
The fog has softened
the sharp edges. The polonaise
of the bald-headed lamps
now begins. With snow
predicted.

Here
the bricks and painted walls
lie exposed, the stairway buckles
and the legion of rats
raises its standards—
pigeon corpses.

Here,
so they say,
a tree shall grow green
and hold the heavens high,
so they say,
with every branch and leaf.

(November 13, 1963)

Kolnoer Tanz

Er tanzt in der Stube,
kleine Schritte im Dielensand,
zittert, wie er den Fuß hebt, sein
Gelächter—ein Leintuch—
stellt sich vor ihn,
vor seine Tränen.

Im Fenster die Pferde
bewegen die Häupter, der Stieglitz
pfeift an den Balken hinauf,
rot und blau die Stockrosen
sagen über den Zaun:
Es kommt ein Regen, bald,
der wird für uns weinen.

Warum weinen, fragt das Gelächter.
Warum lachen, fragen die Tränen.

Ihr macht mir die Füße tanzen,
einer zur Rechten,
einer zur Linken,
beide zur Rechten,
beide zur Linken,
beide voraus auf dem Weg:
wo das Licht weht am Fluß,
fortgeht über die Felder,
auffliegt über dem Wald—

Sprich doch.
Nun spricht er nicht mehr.

Kolno Dance

He dances through the room,
tiny steps on the sandy floorboards,
trembling, he lifts his foot, his
laughter—a linen prayer shawl—
masking
his tears.

The horses at the window
shrug their heads, the goldfinch sends
a trill up to the rafters,
beyond the fence
the red and blue hollyhocks
are saying: The rain will weep for us,
and it's coming soon.

Why cry, asks the laughter.
Why laugh, ask the tears.

You make my feet dance,
skip to the right,
skip to the left,
hop to the right,
hop to the left,
and fling your legs ahead:
to where the light pauses by the river,
then disappears across the fields,
far beyond the woods—

Say something.
Him? He has nothing left to say.

(November 20, 1963)

Der Vogel, weiß

Der Vogel, weiß,
den eine Regung der Luft
hinaustrug über seinen Tod,
der mit fahlen Federn
steht unbeglänzt
über dem Hügel, einer
Birke, über dem eigenen
Schatten. Der Schatten ging
vom Wasser hinauf
auf den Sand.

Es kommt
eine Kirche mit Särgen
unter dem Dach,
mit roten und weißen Steinen
an den Füßen. Es reden
im Laub die Stimmen,
die Münder aus Rauch

von Federn,
von weißen Flügeln,
von einem Vogel Augenlos.

The bird, white

The bird, white,
borne beyond death
by a breath of air,
hangs there, dim,
pale-feathered,
above the hill, above
a birch, above its own
shadow stretched
from the water
to the sands.

Here comes
a church with coffins
beneath its roof,
red and white stones
at its feet. Voices
murmur in the leaves,
their mouths a smoky blur

of feathers,
white wings
of the Eyeless Bird.

(November 26, 1963)

Haus

1.
Da fährt das Licht übers Dach
und will den Amseln nach.
Holunder verwischt auf der Wand
die Linien einer Hand.
Im Rundbeet der Rittersporn
hat aus dem Ohr mich verlorn.
Nun schreibt an das Firstholz der Regen
Hier werd ich mich niederlegen.

2.
An der Wand die Schatten
reden mit Stimmen:
Wie werden wir uns kleiden
für den Tag?

Eine Zitterblume
ins Haar, eine grüne
Ranke über die Augen,
ein Dreiblatt an die Brust.

Schatten, tretet hervor,
das Licht will beginnen mit kleinen
Schritten, zeigt ihm
den Weg.

Den Hang hinunter,
beim Feuergeschrei
der Hähne über die Dächer,
zum alten Gerede der Tiere,

House

1.
Across the roof moves the light
that follows the blackbird's flight.
At the wall the elder trees stand,
blotting out the lines of a hand.
The larkspur in its flower bed
hasn't heard a thing I've said.
Here I'll lay me down, writes the rain
on the ridgepole of a refrain.

2.
Upon the wall, the small talk
of shades:
How shall we dress
for today?

A flower atremble
in the hair, a green tendril
above the eye, a clover-
leaf upon the breast.

Shades, come forward,
the light is ready to take
tiny steps. Help it
on its way.

Down the slope
as the cocks cry fire
across the roofs, the cattle
talk their same old talk,

mit Sprüngen aber,
über den Hofsand.

Schatten, nun geht von der Tür.
Schatten, nun geht von den Fenstern.
Geht hervor unterm Dach.
Schatten Zitterranke,
Weinblatt Schatten, ich will's
hören, Schatten, sprecht:
Du wirst hier bleiben
eine Zeit.

and then lurch
across the sandy yard.

Shades, away from the doors!
Shades, away from the windows!
Away from the rafters!
Shades of tendrils,
shades of vine leaves, let me
hear. O shades, speak:
You'll be here
for a while.

(December 1, 1963)

Wiedererweckung

Das
Land
leer,
durch ausgebreitete Tücher
heraufgrünt das andre, darunter-
gelegte, das ein Verdacht
war
früher. Es kommt
aus der Pestzeit, weiß
von Knochen, Rippen, Wirbeln,
Speichen, vom Kalk.

Zähl
die Gräser
und zähl
Fäden aus Regenwasser,
und Licht, die Blättchen
zähl, und zeichne ein
deine Schritte, Wildspuren,
und Stimmen, beleb
mit Worten
das Blut in den Bäumen und
den Lungen, den Rost
schlag von Wänden
und Stufen,
an deinen Händen
bleibt er, dort mag er sich
nähren
mit deinen Nägeln.

Reawakening

The
land
empty,
and through the field's outspread sheets
that other land, laid out below,
only half suspected
long ago,
rises up, green. It dates
back to the plague, white
with bones, ribs, vertebrae,
radii, lime.

Go count
the grass blades,
go number
the rainwater threads
of light, go count
the tiny leaves and sketch in
your footsteps, spoors
of voice and deer,
and with words
revive
the blood
in lungs and trees,
and from the walls and stairs
rid yourselves
of the rust still stuck
to your hands, waiting
to eat at your nails.

Es ist nicht die Zeit, ihn zu fragen.
Es ist die Zeit für das Wasser
an Halmen, für die erneute
Fügung der Blätter, und Augen
öffne das Laub.

It's not time to ask.
It's time for water to flow
around stalks, for a new
dispensation of leaves, for eyes
to be opened by the green.

(January 12, 1964)

Mit Liedern Sapphos

Aufgeschürzt die haarige
Lippe, von der Insel
schrie wie der Maulesel schreit
die magere Kleine:

    einen peplos,
    safranfarbenen, kränze,
    phrygische, purpur

Solon
vor dem Haus,
wo die Luft umhergeht:
Singt es noch einmal, sagt er,

daß ich erlerne das
Inselgeschrei, die Rufe
über der Erde dicht,
die im verbrannten Kraut,

es erlerne, daß ich
sterb darüber, Worte
hab und Worte, das Sausen,
den Luftzug hinter dem Haupt und,
Worte, über der Brust.

With the Songs of Sappho

From the purse of her furry
lips, out on the isle
this frail little thing
brayed like a mule:

    a peplos,
    saffron-colored, wreaths
    Phrygian, purple

Solon
before the house,
in the circling wind:
Sing it again, he says,

that I might learn more
of island cries, their calls
so thick upon the earth
in the scorch of weeds,

that I might learn
I too could die of this
same rush of song,
winds at my back,
words at my throat.

(February 5, 1964)

Das verlassene Haus

Die Allee
eingegrenzt
mit Schritten Verstorbener. Wie das Echo
über die Luftsee herab
kam, auf dem Waldgrund zieht
Efeu, die Wurzeln
treten hervor, die Stille
naht mit Vögeln, weißen Stimmen.
Im Haus
gingen Schatten, ein fremdes Gespräch
unter dem Fenster. Die Mäuse
huschen
durch das gesprungne Spinett.
Ich sah eine alte Frau
am Ende der Straße
im schwarzen Tuch
auf dem Stein,
den Blick nach Süden gerichtet.
Über dem Sand
mit zerspaltenen harten Blättern
blühte die Distel.
Dort war der Himmel
aufgetan, in der Farbe des Kinderhaars.
Schöne Erde Vaterland.

The Deserted House

The garden path
lined with
the footsteps of the dead. How the echo
drifted down
from the sea of air, ivy grows
on the forest floor, roots
emerge, and in the white
voices of the birds, the silence nears.
Shades shunted about
the house, and beneath the window,
foreign speech. Mice
scurry
through the splintered spinet.
I saw an old woman
at the end of the path
in a black shawl
on the cobbles,
gazing southward.
On the sand
the thistle's stiff split
leaves were in bloom.
And there the sky
unfolded, the color of children's hair.
Vaterland, your earth so fair.

(March 8, 1964)

Alter Hof in Häme

Schöllkraut. Zum Geschrei
der Kuckucke.
Voll Staub
Klette und Nessel.

Die Bretterstufen am Haus.
Aus der Tür
treten die Hölzer.
Spiegellichter tragen
Willkommverse, ausgekramte, Melisse und Aloe.

Rot,
Kavalierhäuschen, rot,
auf dem Absturz des Ufers,
im Fallwind der Schwalben,
rotes Dach, rot
auf dem Wasser.

Wer hier eingeht, hat
einen Namen, er ist übersetzt in drei Sprachen,
zwischen Schläfe und Schläfe
des alten Mannes. Er spricht ihn
hinab auf den See. Eingeschlafen
der künstliche Schwan.
Tote Stimme.

Wie im Gras der Engel
mit zerfressener Hüfte, hölzern, die Spur
Mehl hinter sich,
taub, ohne Rede. Der Rufer

Old Farm in Häme

Saint-John's-wort. With
cuckoo cry.
Full of dust,
burdock, and nettle.

The planks leading up to the house.
The wooden trim of the door.
Lights above the mirrors revealing
welcome verses scratched upon the glass,
Melisse and Aloe.

Red,
the little manor house, red
upon a small eminence by the shore,
downwind from the swallows,
red-roofed, red
above the waters.

Who enters here has
a name, translated into three tongues
by the old man gone gray
at the temples. A name he addresses
to the lake below. The mechanical swan
sound asleep.
Dead voice.

Like the angel in the grass
with its rotted wooden flanks,
a trace of flour in its tracks,
deaf, without a word. The host

hat noch gewartet, die Hand
erhoben, an leerer Scheune
lange.
Dort steht der Holunder.

waited forever, his hand
upheld, at the empty barn. Where
the elder tree grows.

(July 14, 1964)

Vorsorge

Anfälle von Trunksucht.
Sie kommen
wie das Schweigen
kommt.

Die Karte
ist an die Wand genagelt,
unterstrichen ein Name,
die unaufgefundene Stadt,
eingezeichnet
Wege dorthin.

Klette,
treib große Blätter,
verläßlichen Schutz.

Precaution

Drunken
binges
invite
the silence in.

The map
nailed to the wall,
a name underlined,
the city, undiscovered,
yet the roads to it
already charted.

Burdock, spread
your ample leaves,
surefire protection
against disease.

(July 24, 1964)

Undine

Aus ihren Schatten
herauf
die ungesprochene Rede,
aus Blättern
ein gebogener Arm.

Du betrittst eine Brücke.
Du trägst eine Blüte über dem Mund.
Du verbirgst dich an Türmen.
Du wirfst den springenden Kiesel fort.

Feuer habe ich nicht.
Im Stroh die Vögel schlafen.
Hörbar leben im Dach
Flügel und Futterschrei.

        Atem,
trag mich.
        Dunkel,
sprich mit den Händen.
Wassergeräusch baut Nester
in die gefiederte Stille.
Unter dem Wasser die Häuser
halten Türen geöffnet,
Fenster, aus Steinen eine
Treppe tritt vor.

Undine

The unspoken words
emerge
from her shadows,
the curve of her arm
from the leaves.

You step onto a bridge.
You wear a flower on your mouth.
You hide near the towers.
You scatter pebbles with a kick.

I have no fire.
The birds sleep in the straw.
In the eaves, sounds
of wings and feeding cries.

        Breath,
carry me.
        Darkness,
speak with your hands.
Nests are built
in the feathered stillness
by the rushing waters
where the houses
keep their doors and windows open
and the stairs ascend in stone.

(August 26, 1964)

Blutregen

Über uns,
eh sie zu fliegen begannen,
die der Wind hob,
die aufschlugen
gegen den Himmel,
sind ertrunken,
die Blüten,

mit fliegendem Wasser
gefallen,
staubfarben.
Dein Haar ist wie Gras.

Nimm
meinen Atem, der Blut
scheidet
und Wasser,

neue Augenlider
für einen Tag.

Blood Rain

Above us,
before they took flight,
lifted by the wind,
pitched
skyward,
they were drowned,
these blossoms,

plunged into the swift
murk
of the waters.
Your hair is like grass.

Take
my breath, that divides
blood
from water,
fresh eyelids
for a day.

(September 14, 1964)

Entfremdung

Zeit
geht umher
in Kleidern
aus Glück
und Unglück.

Der im Unglück
spricht mit der Klapperstimme
der Störche, die Störche
meiden ihn: sein Gefieder
schwarz, seine Bäume Schatten,
da ist Nacht, seine Wege
gehn in der Luft.

Alienation

Time
moves
this way and that,
clad in good luck
and in bad.

Bad-luck time
clatters like a stork
yet all the storks
avoid him: his plumage
black, his trees shadows,
now that it's night, his every path
up in the air.

(January 31, 1965)

Zu Christoph Meckels Graphiken

Ging auf Händen oder
stand auf der Richtstatt,
Holz, Gerät, die Werkzeuge,
Gegenstände, Flöte und Uhr,
flogen, hingen
an Wolke und Regen, hatten
Hände gekehrt und Stimmen
nach der Erde, Fauchen
zog umher unter ihnen,
Gedächtnis ging nach Verlass'nem
um, das Verlassene irdisch
stand in Dächerfarben
der Häuser schwarz und grün.

Hör,
Stimmen. Was ists?
Erschallt meine eigne Stimme
unter euch? Ihr Flug
aus meiner Schulter, wie Wimper
hinunter und Wasser
auf deiner Wange
unbenannt.

On Christoph Meckel's Graphic Works

Walked on his hands or
stood in the court of law,
wood, utensils, tools,
objects, flutes, clocks
in flight, hanging on to
the clouds and the rain,
hands reaching out, voices
turned earthward, beset
by hissing sounds, in search
of everything left behind
and rediscovered
in the house roofs' earthy
green and blacks.

Listen.
Voices. Of what sort?
Is this my own voice
echoing among you?
It leaps from my shoulder
and like an eyelash
drips a tear down your cheek,
unnamed.

(February 11, 1965)

An Hölty

Maientanz
oder Die Schäferin—
Blättergeschrei um den Lorbeer,
Windung, im Frost
Rauch.
Der Atem
gegangen durch Wasser.

Es war eine Furt,
sandig, Wirbel zogen, das Licht
starr. Es war ein Baum.
Abend. Ein Mund,
der sich dem Salz versagte.

War deine Stimme.
Mailied,
unter der Erde.

To Hölty

May dance
or the Shepherdess—
leaf-cry round the laurel,
whorl, smoke
through frost. Breath
through water.

There was a ford,
sandy, its eddies numb
with light. There was a tree.
Evening. A mouth
that denied itself salt.

Was your voice,
May song,
under earth?

(May 23, 1965)

Das Wort Mensch, als Vokabel

Das Wort Mensch, als Vokabel
eingeordnet, wohin sie gehört,
im Duden:
zwischen Mensa und Menschengedenken.

Die Stadt
alt und neu,
schön belebt, mit Bäumen
auch
und Fahrzeugen, hier

hör ich das Wort, die Vokabel
hör ich hier häufig, ich kann
aufzählen von wem, ich kann
anfangen damit.

Wo Liebe nicht ist,
sprich das Wort nicht aus.

The word "man" as a term

The word "man" as a term
Mensch filed away, where it belongs,
in the Duden dictionary:
between *Mensa* and *Menschengedenken*.
The city, old and new,
O so lively, with all its trees
and means
of transportation, here

I hear the term "man"
so very often, I can number those
who deploy it, so it
just might work for me.

But where love is not,
never utter this word.

(June 15, 1965)

Unpublished Poems

Nachlass

Partisanenwald

Weit die Feuerränder.
Im Kraut verseufzt
Regen. Nimm diesen Weg.

Den du nicht kennst. Eine Rede
geht vor dir her. Du wirfst
einen Schatten aus Raschellaut.

Vogelruf. Über dem Fluß
Antwort. Um dich der Kreis
abgeschritten, ein Tierpfad,
durch die Farne
und auf den Wassern schon.

Über dem Feuer,
hör, mit dem scharfen Fluge,
über den Wind hinauf
fahren die Vögel.

Partisan Woods

Distant gunfire at forest's edge.
Rain breathes its last
in the weeds. Take this path.

Unknown to you. You hear
talking. You cast
the rustle of a shadow.

Bird cries. An answer
from across the river. You survey
your surroundings, animal
tracks leading to the water
through the ferns.

Over the gunfire,
listen to the sliced flight
of birds as they drive
against the wind.

(1954)

An Heloise

Auf der Wand dein Gesicht,
ein wenig
Kohle und Rouge.

Und du sprichst, wenn es dunkelt,
das Vergessene. So
sangen Sibyllen sommers. Abend
fiel auf ihr Haar, ihr Mund
klang weich, ein wenig dunkler
schien er am Bogenrand.

Die geborstene Schläfe
über dem Wangenschatten
sahen wir nicht.

To Héloïse

Your face on the wall,
a bit of kohl
and rouge.

And you speak, as the dark
takes hold, of everything forgotten. Thus
the sibyls sang in summertime. Evening
fell upon their hair, their tongue
sounding soft, though somewhat darker
at the rainbow's edge.

How the blood burst from their temples
and flowed down the shadows of their cheeks
escaped our notice.

(January 21, 1956)

Nachtlied

Vogel, komm,
grüner Vogel,
hoch aus dem Sternbild komm,
unter mein Laubdach, Vogel,
wir reden mitsammen

von den Ufern atmender
Ströme, der schwarzen Erde
im Waldland,
der Götter Haus,

wo sich der Mensch beginnt,
über sich sieht er das Licht,
findets im andern
Aug: so lernt er zu singen.

Vogel,
grüner Vogel,
unter dem Laubdach laß uns
reden davon.

Night Song

Bird, come here,
green bird, come
down from the starry skies
beneath my arbor, bird,
let's converse

about the banks of the breathing
rivers, about the woodlands'
black soil, about the home
of the gods

where man has his beginnings
and sees the light above
and finds it in another's
eye, thus learning to sing.

Bird,
green bird,
under this canopy of leaves,
let's converse.

(May 19, 1956)

September

Nun ist ein Dunkel,
weit,
über die Stunde herab
wehend. Du willst nicht gehn.
Blaß die Rosen, noch
die Aster
am Zaun herauf,
blau und der Dämmrung
Gebild.

Und wir werden einander
lieben, in jeden Morgen
setzen den Schritt, die weißen
Lieder rufen aus Schnee,
laut
und die Brust
voller Sommer,
Küsse im Nacken, Singsang
der Grillen im Haar.

September

Now the breadth
of darkness
breathes upon the hour.
You choose to stay.
The roses, pale, then
the aster upon
the lattice, blue,
shape
of dusk.

And we shall love each other
and set foot in every
dawn, our white
songs calling out
from the snow,
our lungs filled
with summer, kisses
at our napes, cricket calls
round our hair.

(June 7, 1956)

1943

Du sahst
den Elch im niederen
Ufergeländ, aus den Nebeln
taucht er im frühen Jahr,
auf den Schaufeln
regentönend
trägt er die Nacht.

Und die Eulen
hörtest du und die Taube
nah überm Forst, der Sommer
schallt übers Moor,

da wir gegangen
die kleine Zeit vor dem Abschied,
unter der Luft aus schlagenden Flügeln,
da wir gerufen
über den Fluß. Bei den Schultern
hielt ich dich an.

Später
kehr ich zurück.
Ich verlerne das Dunkel.
In Küssen, einmal, wie ist das
um die Stirn mir gekommen:
Rauch aus den Gärten, Raute,
leichter Atem der Bitternis.

1943

You saw the elk
on the low coastal
plain, it emerges
from the mists every spring,
carrying the night
upon its antlers
spattered with rain.

And you heard the owls
and the pigeons
above the woods, the echo
of summer over the marsh

where we briefly walked
before saying our goodbyes
amid all the wing-thrash overhead,
calling out
over the river. I held you
by your shoulders.

Later
I return.
I unlearn the dark.
As we kissed, how did this
cross my mind? Smoke rose
from the gardens, rue,
slight whiff of bitterness.

(June 18, 1956)

Trakl

Als ein Blitz
fuhr der Tag nieder
über dem Wasser.

Unter der Tür
stand der Schwester Schatten.
Die Schwalbenflucht hob an.

Trakl

Like lightning
the day fell
upon the water.

The sister's shadow
stood beneath the door.
The swallows broke into flight.

(March 24, 1954)

Trakl

Stirn.
Der braune Balken. Totenuhren
zermürben den Nachmittag.

Flieder. Spät der Wein,
lang um ein Licht
dunstend. Der Morgen voll Tau.

Wann schlug dein Blick auf? Wer kam
vom Dorf in den Hügeln herab?
Kam mit dem Mond?

Licht lag im Fenster,
ein bleierner Rand um die Rede
bebend verwarteter Nacht.
—
Bebender Sommer. Die Nähe
der weißen Zeit, in der Schwalben
wirrem Geschrei.

Trakl

Brow.
The brown beam. Dead hours
erode the afternoon.

Lilacs. Late the wine,
late to release its savor
to the light. Mornings nothing but dew.

When did the eyes open? Who
came down from the hillside village?
Did he come with the moon?

The light lay in the window,
across all the leaded stained-glass window talk,
tremors, angst, awaiting night.
—
Summer tremors. White times
in the offing, swallows'
bewildered cries.

(March 19, 1958)

Trakl

Stirn.
Der braune Balken.
Dielenbretter. Die Schritte
zum Fenster.
Das Grün großer Blätter. Zeichen,
geschrieben über den Tisch.

Die splitternde Schwelle. Und
verlassen. Langsam
hinter dem Fremdling her
unter Flügeln der Dohlen
in Gras und Staub
die Straße ohne Namen.

Trakl

Brow.
The brown beam.
Floorboards. Footsteps
toward the window.
The broad-leaved green. Signs
scrawled above the table.

The doorsill splintering. Then
abandoned. While the stranger
makes his slow escape
amid the jackdaw wings,
leaving the nameless street
in the dust.

(May 29, 1964)

*An * * **

Ich zerdrück
ein Jahr in den Händen. Was weiß ich?
Du kommst mit der provençalischen Zeit,
durch die Wälder
bist du gekommen,
um einen dunstenden See,
als niemals Tag war.

Damals, eine zierliche
Spur an der Furt auf dem Sandweg,
die das jüdische Mädchen
eintrat im Lauf—den gesenkten
Scheitel, des Händlers Stock—des Rasainer
Müllers Abendgered, wenn der Nebel
stieß an den Zaun—
das
weiß ich
und wie der Strom um den Berg zog, die Ebene
füllte, als schriee der Fluren
verwitterter Gott von den Hügeln—
schwankende Schatten
unzähligen Todes
trag ich dir zu.

Und du sagst: Die Spur
ist verwachsen, die Rede
tönt nicht mehr um den Abend,
gemordet ist Wronka,
deutest auf diesen und den,
Gründe zählst du, du sagst:
So ist es gewesen.—

To * * *

I stub out
a year in my palms. What do I know?
You arrive with your "Provençal Intermezzo,"
you came
through the woods
around a misty lake
where the sun never shone.

Back then, the faint
trace by the ford on the sandy path
that the Jewish girl discovered
on the run—the sunken
trace of a merchant's cane—the Raseiniai
miller's evening gossip, when the fog
drifted up against the fence—
this
I know
and how the river flowed around the mountain and seeped
into the plain as if the weathered god of the fields
had cried out from the hills—
to you I now propose
the shifting shadows
of the uncounted dead.

And you say: The trace
she left is now overgrown, no more
evening gossip to be heard,
Wronka lies murdered,
and making this and that clear,
detailing the various reasons, you conclude:
So it goes.

Sag,
von dir muß ichs hören:
Es wird nie mehr so sein.

Say it,
I need to hear it from you:
This will never happen again.

(February 1958)

Memorial

Schwarz vor den Horizont
geschüttet, die Stadt. Ich zähl die Gewitter
über ihr. Morgen geh ich, ich will ein Grab
schließen, verlassen wie diese
Stadt, die zerstört ist
bis in den Grund, die die Vögel
meiden. Ein Baum
steht mir am Weg. Der gibt mir
von seinem Laub.

Memorial

The city, black, spilled out
from the horizon. I count the thunderstorms
overhead. Tomorrow I'm off to close up
a grave, abandoned
like this city, razed
to the ground, avoided
by the birds. There's a tree
along my way. It'll offer me
leaves.

(August 22, 1959)

Im Mühlenwind

Küsse. Der eine ein Riß
über die Brust, "gefallen
bin ich, gestürzt, meine Birke aus Schneelicht".
    Der andre
schwer, Regenlaut, eh es tagt.

Dann
nie mehr ein Wort:
heute. Immer nur, immer
gestern nur, gestern.

Bald,
wenn der Schwan
ruft, heraufährt
unter der Wolke und glänzt,
steh ich, die Sichel gelegt um den Nacken,
im Mühlenwind
geh ich davon.

In the Millwind

Kisses. One of which ripped
through my breast: "I have fallen
hard, my snow-lit birch." The other
kiss heavy, sound of rain, before dawn.

Then
no longer a word:
today. On and on, yesterday
come and gone.

Soon,
when the swan
calls and rises up
in splendor beneath the cloud,
I'll stand, sickle to my neck,
in the millwind,
and take my leave.

(October 2, 1959)

Andenken an Hölderlin

Einmal ein Land,
gestorbenes Blut, die Felder
der Bretagne. Auf einen Stein
gelehnt, die ruhlose Stimme
hören der Dämmerung.
Oder den Baum aus Vogelgeschrei
auf dem Meer.

Einmal, die Oka hinab
und die Wolga, das Herz der Flüsse
weiß in der frühen Nacht,
Kljasma und Nerlj. Der Ufersturz von Wladimir
unter dem alten Gold
der Mauern und Türme. Im Wind.

Dort ein Mädchen,
das nach den Tieren blickt.
Eine Mütze über der Hecke.
Dort der junge Fischer.
Das treibende Boot. An dem Torbau
die Greisin zuletzt.

Leicht ist der Vogel den Lüften,
noch seine Angst
hält ihn im Licht.
Wir reden mit halber Stimme:
Geh und grüße
die schöne Garonne.

In Memory of Hölderlin

There was once a blood-
dimmed land, the fields
of Brittany. Leaning on
their giant stones, the restless voices
lent an ear to dusk.
Or to the boughs of birdcall
by the sea.

Once, down the Oka
and the Volga, the heart of those rivers
white in the early night,
the Klyazma and the Neri. The landslide in Vladimir
over those ancient golden
walls and towers. In the wind.

A young girl there
peering at the animals.
A cap flipped over the hedge.
The young fisherman there.
The boat pressing ahead. And at long last,
the old woman at the gate.

The bird frail upon the breeze,
held aloft in the light
by fear.
With half a voice we say:
"Go and greet
the sweet Garonne."

(October 1959)

Rabelais

Jetzt
der Weingarten hier,
diese Mauer, ich kann
lehnen am Stein, dem Apfelbaum
reiche ich ins Geäst.

Damals
beim Drucker, wir druckten
Bücher, es steht darin,
was alle Welt weiß
wie die Sorbonne und nicht besser.

So dacht ich, es müßt wie ein Teufel
schreiben die linke Hand,
sie schreibt auch, ich kenn einen Strom,
treibende Bäume, zerbrochne
Zäune voll toter Fische,
der mich ersäuft, der die Brust
einstößt, Magen, Milz, Nieren—den Strom.

Weither aber kommt
besegelt der Himmel, ich will
die Beschreibung lesen vorzeitig
meines Lebens, die einer gibt:
er sieht das Land nicht, er steht
im Kohlfeld mit engen Augen
und geht davon auf der See.

Ich warte, im Tor, vor der schönen
Treppe, der Garten ist hell:

Rabelais

Now
this vineyard,
this stone wall
on which to lean, this apple tree
branch within reach.

Back then
at the printers we'd bring out
books containing
what the world knows every bit
as well as the Sorbonne, and no better.

So I thought my devilish left hand
might well manage the following
scrawl: I know of a river,
trees asway, broken
weirs full of dead fish, which
drowns me, smashing my chest,
belly, kidneys, spleen—the river.

But then heaven swoops down
on its sails, I'd like to read someone's
account of my life
ahead of time:
he's blind to the lie of the land,
just stands there in the coalfield, narrow-eyed,
then makes his way to the sea.

I wait at the gate, at the foot
of these fine stairs, the garden bright

im Wind mit den Vogelflügen
silbern
der Tag von Thelem.

and the bird wings in the wind
silver
at the dawn of Thélème.

(1960–1961)

Stadtbesuch

Die alte Ausfallstraße—
Einfallstraße wär besser.
Jeder kommt dort herein.
Der Alte kennt Heide und Luch.
Er trägt einen kleinen Hut.

Keiner fragt ihn. Er fragt nicht.
Er findet Altes. Apoll
streicht um den Bahnhof
um einen Jungen. Demeter
keimt im Gewölbe Kartoffeln
ab. An der Mauer steht: Du
gehe bei Frieda. Komme nicht mehr.

Um die neuen Häuser
Nacht. Aus Licht und Geräusch.
Auf einer Bank.
Morgen dem Vogel folgt er,
die alte Einfallstraße—
Ausfallstraße wär besser.

City Tour

The old escape route
or, more aptly, invasion route.
They all pour in from there.
The old man knows of meadow and mire.
A little hat upon his head.

No one asks him. Nor does he ask.
He discovers ancient things. Apollo
haunts the railway station
in search of a youth. Demeter
sprouts potatoes under the arches.
Scrawled on a wall: Have a go
at Frieda. Scram. Don't come back.

Around the newly built houses,
night. Full of light and noise.
On a bench. Tomorrow
he'll follow the bird.
The old escape route—
invasion route would be more apt.

(March 16, 1960)

Rosa Luxemburg

Schmerz
wie ein Vogel singt.
Mauer. Lüfte, hörbar
über der Angst.

Wer verschließt deinen Mund,
Lerche? Du fliegst
auf vom Wiesenstädtchen,
in die Verwüstung, vorüber
Türmen, atemlos, dort:

Lerche, sing deinem Volk,
sing der Schläfen
Gewalt. Ich hör einen Alten
reden von finsteren Jahren.
Zärtlichkeit, eine Träne,
sagt deinen Namen.

Rosa Luxemburg

The pain
whenever any bird sings.
Wall. The winds within hearing
over the fear.

Lark, who locks
your mouth as you soar up
from the small meadow towns
into the devastation, over
the towers, out of breath?

Lark, sing of your people,
of the power apulse in their temples.
I hear an old man
talk of the dark days.
In tears, tenderness
speaks your name.

(March 25, 1960)

Steh. Sprich. Die Stimme

Steh. Sprich. Die Stimme
nicht, die singende
nicht. Die andere, die das Gras
niederlegt. Das Insekt
schließt seine Flügel zusammen
mitten im Flug,

wirbelt, ein Blatt. Die andre
Stimme: Wollflies, Gehörn,
Klauen. Der Rost
geht auf dem Sand, der Fels
bricht aus dem Grund.

Redende Stimme. Wo Angst
eingegraben war, fliegen
Blätter, geädert
mit splitternden Fäden, Eis
fliegt, eine Hand
fängt es im Flug.

Unwirsch Liebe, verwischt
mit der Hand: die Zeichnung,
die den Regen nicht übersteht,
Regen wird, fliegend,
aufschlägt
gegen den Wind.

Stand. Speak.

Stand. Speak. Not with
this voice, the one that sings. But with
this other voice, beneath
the grass. In midflight
the insect
folds its wings,

whirls, a leaf. This other
voice: fleece, antlers,
claws. The rust that seeps
into the sand, the stone
that bursts from the ground.

This speaking voice. Where fear
lay buried, leaves
now glide, veined with
splintered threads. Ice
takes to the air, caught on the fly
by a hand.

Quarrelsome love, wiped away
by the back of the wrist: a sketch
that won't survive the rain,
the rain, aflight,
hits up
against the wind.

JONA KOMM
WIR REDEN UND REDEN
SAG NINIVE
SAG MORGEN MORGEN MORGEN

JONAH COME
WE TALK AND TALK
SAY NINEVEH
SAY TOMORROW TOMORROW TOMORROW

(July 8, 1964)

Klagemauer

Gezogen
vor unsere Münder, vor
die Schwärze unserer Augen, geneigt
gegen die Nägel an unseren Händen, Mauer,

deren Höhe das Windlicht hält
über die Schatten, keiner
nimmt es herab.

Daniel trat vor die Wand.
Wir lesen Zeichen, eisern
die Feuer, Daniels Stimme
tönt, wir erschrecken nicht.

Wailing Wall

Laid out
before our mouths, before
the black of our eyes, rammed
into our fingernails. Wall, whose

heights bear the wind's light
over the shadows, no one dares
tear you down.

Daniel stood at the Wall.
We read signs, irons
in the fire. Daniel's voice
rings out. We feel no fear.

(1961–1963)

Fragmente

Der folgt dir, jener—
und du kehrst nicht um.

Gesicht
Schlaf, einen Stein
geädert

Liebe ist eine Gestalt
kein Laut wird dich rufen

Die Nacht
ein Grün,
drei Blätter,
eine rote Beere

Ich bau ein Haus
für unsere Augen

Fragments

Someone is following you—
yet you don't turn around.

(March 1962)

Face

Sleep, a stone
with veins

(March 1962)

Night,
green,
three leaves,
a red berry

I'm building a house
for our eyes

(1965)

Notes

Sarmatian Time (1961)

CALL

The German title, "Anruf," can also suggest an invocation or telephone call.

Vilna: Or Vilnius (in Lithuanian) or Wilno (in Polish), from the thirteenth to the late eighteenth century the capital of the Grand Duchy of Lithuania and later of the Polish-Lithuanian Commonwealth, one of the largest states in early modern Europe. Subsequently occupied by various Russian, French, German, Polish, and Soviet regimes, before reverting back to Lithuania. Here addressed as an oak, the sacred cosmic tree associated with the Baltic thunder god Perkūnas.

Novgorod: Legendary Russian town, founded in the ninth century by the Vikings (who called it Holmgard). A major way station on the Baltic-to-Byzantium amber route (via the rivers Volkhov, Lovat, and Dnieper) and the capital of Kievan Rus'. Alexander Nevsky defeated the Teutonic Knights near here in 1242. Embodied by the birch, a traditional symbol of the Russian homeland.

NYMPH

bleeding / herb: Identified by Bobrowski as Saint-John's-wort.

Syrinx: Chaste nymph who, fleeing Pan's lecherous attentions, called out in fright to her river sisters to transform her into a reed. Pan, frustrated and grief-stricken, later transformed the reed into the panpipe or syrinx on which he played his rustic songs of lust and loss.

CHILDHOOD

Men stepped / into the room, calling out to their dogs / over their shoulders: These lines have been compared to those in Paul Celan's "Todesfuge" ("Deathfugue"): "a man lives in the house your golden hair Margarete / he sets his dogs on us he gifts us a grave in the air" (trans. Pierre Joris).

TO THE JEWISH PEDDLER A.S.

Raseiniai: One of the earliest Jewish communities established in western Lithuania, known in Yiddish as Raseyn and the center of the Haskalah movement.

THE ANCIENT ARMY ROUTE

this Corsican: Napoleon, in retreat from Moscow in 1812 across Lithuania and Poland.

WAGON TRIP

Mariampol: German-Jewish-Lithuanian town near the East Prussian border. Site of major massacres and deportations of its minorities under Nazi and subsequent Soviet occupations.

THE LOG CABIN ABOVE THE RIVER VILIA

Vilia: The river (Neris in Lithuanian) that flows by Vilna before joining the Memel near Kaunas to the south.

Friend... let us sing: In imitation of the Finnish folk epic *Kalevala*, which Bobrowski owned in Martin Buber's 1921 German translation.

Alinka: Polish pet name for Alicia.

VILNA

Gediminas: Grand duke of Lithuania and legendary founder of Vilna who in the early fourteenth century fought off the Teutonic Knights from the west and the Poles and Tartars from the east.

Nieman: Polish name for the river Nemanus (in Lithuanian) or Memel (in German).

Mickiewicz: See the opening strophes of part 4 of Adam Mickiewicz's 1834 epic, *Pan Tadeusz*, where he also mentions the legendary Lithuanian bard Lizdeika. Mickiewicz lived in Vilna during his youth.

Trakai: Ancient castle built by Gediminas on an island in a lake near Vilna.

your Jews: Vilna had since the fifteenth century been a traditional hub of Jewish life and learning, known as the "Jerusalem of the North." In June 1941, when the Germans invaded Lithuania, approximately 60,000 Jews (or 30 percent of the total population of the town) lived there, half of whom were shot and buried in mass graves. Two years later, the remainder were similarly massacred or sent to the Sobibor extermination camp or deported to labor camps in Estonia and Latvia. Over 90 percent of the Jewish population of Vilna died in World War II.

BY THE RIVER

Ostra Bama: Late Northern Renaissance icon of the Virgin, displayed in the Chapel of the Gate of Dawn in Vilna.

GRAVEYARD

Mouths stuffed with grass: Plays on the German vernacular *ins Gras beißen* (bite the dust).

DEAD LANGUAGE

The title refers to Old Prussian, a language nearly extinct by the eighteenth century. From an ancient dictionary in his possession, Bobrowski transcribed into his notebooks a number of its surviving words. Here: *laurio* (water), *warne* (crow), *wittan* (meadow), *smordis* (buckthorn).

THE TRACE IN THE SAND

A response to the first section of Paul Celan's 1952 collection *Mohn und Gedächtnis* (*Poppy and Memory*), entitled "Sand from the Urns."

LITHUANIAN SONGS

The unrhymed quatrains follow the form of traditional Lithuanian folk songs, or *dainos*.

THE SARMATIAN PLAIN

Refers to the area lying between the Vistula and the Volga and the Caspian Sea, empire of the ancient Scythians, and here imagined as extending southeast into the realm of Ishtar, the Mesopotamian goddess of war and sexual love, associated with the planet Venus.

COUNTERLIGHT

The title of the third section of Celan's *Poppy and Memory*. Compare Hölderlin's poem "Tinian": "There are flowers / Not engendered by the earth, sprouting / From loose soil of their own accord,/ Day's counterlight, it is not / Proper to pick these, / For they stand golden, / Unprepared, / Without leaves, / Like thoughts."

PRUZZIAN ELEGY

The pagan Old Prussians, worshippers of nature gods, inhabited the southeastern shore of the Baltic Sea between the Vistula Lagoon to the west and the Curonian Lagoon to the east. They were gradually exterminated as a people or Christianized as a culture by the Teutonic Knights over the course of the thirteenth and fourteenth centuries. It is estimated that between 1230 and 1283, some 80,000 Old Prussians (or 33 percent of the population) were killed; the rest eventually died out or were assimilated into the cultures of their German (or Slavonic) invaders. This breakthrough poem of 1952 was not included in the original West German edition of *Sarmatian Time* in 1961 because one of its in-house readers objected to its repeated use of the controversial (and Nazi-tinged) word *Volk*.

Perkūns: Or Perkūnas, an Old Prussian Baltic god of the sky and thunder, portrayed as a stern figure with a crown of flames.

Peckols: Or Picollos, a white-bearded Baltic god of the underworld.

Patrimpas: Or Potrimpos, the Baltic god of fertility and good fortune, pictured as wearing a wreath of wheat ears on his head.

the fisherman: Perkūns in his guise as fisher king?

VILLON

Accused of theft and banished from Paris in1463, the French poet François Villon spent his final years wandering through France. Bobrowski has him ending up near Calais, where he himself was briefly stationed with the Wehrmacht in 1940.

silent martyr: Not only the exiled poète maudit Villon but also the local fish known as John Dory, Saint Pierre's fish, or Peter's fish.

GÓNGORA

Inspired by Bobrowski's discovery of Federico García Lorca's 1927 speech in praise of the seventeenth-century Spanish poet Luis de Góngora—whose baroque-modernist imagery Lorca recommended to the contemporary (Andalusian) Generation of 1927 writers. Legend has it that Góngora went mad and died because of his fellow poet Quevedo's persecutions.

JOSEPH CONRAD

Bobrowski was proud to claim Józef Teodor Konrad Korzeniowski (1857–1924) as a distant relative, Conrad's mother, Ewa, having been a Bobrowski. After the death of his parents at age eleven, Conrad was given over to the care of his mother's brother, Tadeusz Bobrowski.

Here the coast / gleams fever-green: Bobrowski's favorite Conrad novel was his 1914 *The Shadow-Line,* whose Gulf of Siam setting may be refracted in this poem.

Chernigov: A city in northern Ukraine. Conrad returned to his native Poland three times: in 1890 (before departing for the Congo), then in 1893 and again in 1914.

Dniester: A river in northwestern Ukraine, near the Polish region where Conrad grew up.

DYLAN THOMAS

Marlais: Welsh for "martyr" and the middle name of Swansea-born Dylan Thomas. Bobrowski wrote this five years after the poet's death in New York City, having read accounts of his drunken reading tours through the United States. Many of the motifs in the poem derive from Thomas's BBC radio drama, *Under Milk Wood*, which aired posthumously in 1954.

THE WHOOPER SWAN

Song of Igor's Campaign: Russian national epic telling of the unsuccessful campaign of Prince Igor of Novgorod-Seversky against the Kumans, a Turkic nomadic people inhabiting the lands above the Black Sea and along the Volga.

VILLAGE ROAD

Ryazan: An ancient city, 200 kilometers southeast of Moscow on the Oka river.

Mikula: Mythical Russian plowman of giant strength, celebrated in early song.

Chaadayev: Pyotr Chaadayev (1794–1856), Russian philosopher, cultural critic, and friend of Pushkin.

THE CHURCH

"Assuage My Sorrows": A common Russian prayer addressed to icons endowed with healing powers.

Our Lady of the Fields: Identified by Bobrowski as an ancient Slavic vegetation goddess.

ON THE TAURIC ROAD

The road leading to Taurida, also known as Little Tartary, the site of the Crimean Khanate, self-declared successors to the Golden Horde (1441–1783).

Enkidu: The hero of the Assyrian-Babylonian epic *Gilgamesh*.

LANDSCAPE WITH BIRDS

Temujin: The Mongol Genghis Khan, whose empire reached as far west as the Caspian Sea.

seven men: The Seven Sleepers of legend were a group of Christian youths who hid in a cave around 250 CE to escape from Roman persecution and who fell into a miraculous slumber for two hundred years—only to awake to find Christianity finally legalized.

LAKE ILMEN 1941

As a member of the German army's signal corps, Bobrowski was stationed in the vicinity of this 380-square-mile lake just south of Novgorod between the early summer of 1941 and the late fall of 1943. He observed: "I began writing at Lake Ilmen in 1941, about the Russian landscape, but as a German." This revisiting of his first impressions of the lake (the twenty-fifth version of a 1941 poem, he admitted to a friend) is dated June 1959, nearly two decades later.

RIVER POEM

Inspired by Friedrich Hölderlin's hymns to the Rhine and the Danube. Bobrowski noted that in this poem he wanted to create a composite image of the course of the rivers Düna and Volga.

calamus: The rush or sedge known as calamus occurs frequently in Bobrowski's poetry. Mentioned in the Bible as a source of incense or anointing oil, it traditionally symbolized sweetness and purity. In Roman times it served as the name for their reed pens. For its further phallic associations, see the "Calamus" section of Walt Whitman's *Leaves of Grass*.

THE PAINTER CHAGALL'S HOMELAND

The Jewish painter Marc Chagall was born in 1887 near Vitebsk (in today's Belarus). The grandfather (fiddling?) on the roof comes from Chagall's 1931 autobiography.

those stars that seeded: See Exodus 32:13.

LATVIAN SONGS

my father the hawk: Here, as elsewhere in his poetry, the hawk may allude to one of the ancestral branches of the Bobrowski family named Jastrzebiec ("hawk" in Polish).

the white / lord: Metonym for the Teutonic Knights in their white cloaks and black crosses?

Uexküll: Bobrowski explains this nobleman's crime as follows: "A Herr von Uexküll appeared before the city council in Riga in the seventeenth century, charged with murdering one of his servants." Hegel's lord and bondsman.

THE DÜNA

Düna: The Daugava River, also known as the Western Dvina or Väina River, rises close to the source of the Volga in Russia, and then flows through Belarus and Latvia into the Gulf of Riga on the Baltic Sea. Bobrowski was stationed by this river in the spring and summer of 1944 and was later captured at nearby Kandava by the Russians on May 8, 1945, the last day of the war.

KAUNAS 1941

Kaunas, the second-largest town in Lithuania, was located at the confluence of the Neris (Vilia) and the Nemunas (Memel) Rivers, its population 20 percent Jewish. During his youth Bobrowski had visited relatives there who published a local German-language newspaper in what was then known as Memelland. Later, as a signal corpsman in the Wehrmacht, he witnessed the pogrom in which German Einsatzgruppen, aided by Lithuanian collaborators, slaughtered 3,800 Jews on June 28, 1941. Several months thereafter, the Germans killed another 10,000. This poem is dated June 1958, exactly seventeen years after the first Kaunas pogrom.

RETURN

Bobrowski called this his most personal poem—memories of childhood holidays on his grandparents' farm in Motzischken on the banks of the River Jura in southwestern Lithuania.

ONE DAY

Let me linger awhile: See John 13:33.

THE MEMEL

The ancient German name of the river that since the early fifteenth century had traditionally defined the eastern boundary between the kingdoms of Germany and Lithuania. The Jura, Mitva, and Szezupe are its tributaries.

THE DAUBAS

Lithuanian name for the left bank of the Memel near Ragnit—today part of the Russian Kaliningrad Oblast—and frequent scene of Bobrowski's childhood reveries.

Where then / should we reside?: After Hölderlin's poem "Der Adler" ("The Eagle"): "*wo denn / wollen wir bleiben?*"

your daughters' hair: At the time of this writing, Bobrowski's daughters were two and three.

REFUSAL

The German title, "Absage," can also be translated as renunciation or rejection—or as the closing announcement or sign-off at the end of a radio program. The first lines of the poem have sometimes been read as sarcastically referring to those perfect red-blooded specimens of Communist manhood celebrated by GDR propaganda—in which, by late 1959, Bobrowski had ceased to believe.

Perkūns: See the final lines of "Pruzzian Elegy."

The new has never begun: See Ecclesiastes 1:9: "there is no new thing under the sun."

age without fear: Possible nod to W. H. Auden's 1947 poem "The Age of Anxiety."

Shadowland Rivers (1963)

THE EAGLE

Traditional symbols of the Ascension of Christ, spread eagles were often nailed onto local doors as sacred hunting trophies endowed with magical properties. See Bobrowski's favorite Hölderlin poem, "The Eagle."

DRYAD

Dryads are classical nymphs that live—and eventually expire—with their host trees: the laurel, the oak, the ash, and here, the northern birch.

TALE

Kitezh: According to a thirteenth-century Russian legend, the Christian city of Kitezh, under attack by the Mongol ruler Batu Khan, suddenly became invisible and sank into a lake. Evoked in a poem by the Russian poet Sergei Yesenin (1895–1925), which Bobrowski read in Celan's translation.

THE WANDERER

open / doors: See Matthew 7:7, "Ask, and it shall be given you; seek, and ye shall find; knock, and it shall be opened unto you."

HAMANN

The speaker of this cento of quotes from his diaries and letters is Bobrowski's great culture hero Johann Georg Hamann (1730–1788), born in Königsberg and known as "the Magus of the North." Bobrowski's own notes to the poem run: "*Wasianski*: then priest to the local Polish congregation. The author of *Lives According to a*

Rising Line was Th. G. Hippel; the author of *Poems in the Style of Grécourt* was J. G. Scheffner; both books were published anonymously. *Lizentgraben*: where Hamann lived. *Katzbach*: where he was born."

Wasianski: Ehregott Andreas Christoph Wasianski (1755–1831), Königsberg theologian and amanuensis to Immanuel Kant. Narrator of Thomas De Quincey's *The Last Days of Immanuel Kant.*

With Sancho I repeat: See *Don Quixote*, part II, chapter 5.

ELDER BLOSSOM

Isaac Babel: Twentieth-century Russian writer, born in Odessa in 1894 and died in the Gulag in 1940 during the Stalinist purges. The anecdote is taken from his 1925 "The Story of My Dovecote," which tells of the October 1905 pogrom that swept through nearby Nikolaev, killing his grandfather as well as destroying his own dovecote, one of whose birds was snatched from him, its head cut off and its bloody entrails smashed against his face. The elder blossom (or *Holunder)* of the title is taken from an 1863 story by Wilhelm Raabe, which refers to the profuse flowering of the elderberry bush in the old Jewish cemetery of Prague in memory of the dead.

TO BARKAN THE HASSID

Bobrowski was a great admirer of Martin Buber's *Tales of the Hasidim* (1946).

where the harps / hung from the willow trees: See Psalm 137:1–2: "By the rivers of Babylon, there we sat down, yea, we wept, when we remembered Zion. We hanged our harps upon the willows in the midst thereof."

to sow in tears: See Psalm 126:5.

NÄNIE

German form of the Latin *naenia*, or funeral ode—as in the title of Friedrich Schiller's celebrated lament, later set to music by Johannes Brahms.

Helsingør: The Elsinore of Hamlet, where the Danish composer Dieterich Buxtehude served as the organist at Saint Olaf's Church early in his career (1660–1668).

concentus: The part of a church service (for example, hymn or psalm) intoned by the whole choir.

the rainbow: Friedrich Gottlieb Klopstock's 1759 ode "The Celebration of Spring" (beloved by Werther's Lotte) closes with the rainbow that God sent after the Flood as a sign of his renewed covenant with humanity.

FRENCH VILLAGE

Here comes Martin: Patron saint of France whose feast day, marking the end of the harvest season and the beginning of winter, is celebrated on November 11th.

BRENTANO IN ASCHAFFENBURG

The town in which the German poet and folk-song collector Clemens Brentano (1778–1842) spent the latter years of his life. Celebrates Bobrowski's invitation in late 1960 to join the yearly meeting of the West German Gruppe 47 at his house.

"Alas, without sacrifice": A line from one of Brentano's poems.

HÖLDERLIN IN TÜBINGEN

Occasioned by Bobrowski's participation in a meeting of the Hölderlin Society in spring 1961. The Swabian poet spent the final decades of his life (1807–1843) in a tower near Tübingen overlooking the Neckar river, under the care of a local carpenter. The final lines of the poem echo Hölderlin's "Hälfte des Lebens" ("Half of Life"): "The walls stand cold / And speechless, in the wind / The weathervanes creak."

OF RIVERS

Ce n'était pas assez...: "It was not enough that so many seas, it was not enough that so many countries had scattered the course of our years." From Saint-John Perse's 1944 poem "Neiges." The remainder of the poem rehearses images from Perse's life and works: his travels through the Gobi desert (in *Anabase*) and memories of his childhood in the Antilles (in *Éloges*).

BIRD ROUTES 1957

Väinämöinene: Hero of the national Finnish epic, *Kalevala*.

a new sun / flares forth: Alludes to that summer's atomic bomb tests in the Pacific by the Western powers, said to have disrupted the migratory routes of birds.

GERTRUD KOLMAR

German Jewish poet (1894–1943), deported and murdered at Auschwitz, whose entrance gate bore the inscription Arbeit macht Frei ("Work makes free"). The final two lines quote her poem "The Jewess," its encircling towers perhaps signifying the bastions of Jewish faith that provide protection against persecution.

ELSE LASKER-SCHÜLER

German Jewish poet (1869–1945) who fled Nazi Germany for Jerusalem in 1939.

Przemyśl, Brzozów... Mielec: Small towns in southeastern Poland, sites of Jewish deportation, extermination, and slave labor during World War II, possibly first encountered while Bobrowski was stationed in Poland in 1939.

out of the furnaces: See Daniel 3:25–27.

TO NELLY SACHS

German Nobel laureate, Jewish poet (1891–1970) who fled Nazi Germany in 1940 for Sweden. Bobrowski visited her in Stockholm in 1964. Composed in 1961, this poem is a response to Celan's poem dedicated to Sachs, "Zurich, at the Stork Inn," published the previous year, commemorating their brief meeting in Switzerland, where both were struck by a visionary gleam across the lake on Ascension Day—in the post-Shoah absent presence of God.

Foxes have holes: Matthew 8:20.

Perun: Slavic god of thunder, whose wooden idol was desecrated and thrown into the Dnieper River in 998 by Vladimir the Great as part of his forced conversion of the pagan Kievan Rus'.

his birds, / quick of heart, / have a nest: See Psalm 84:3: "Yea, the sparrow hath found an house, and the swallow a nest for herself, where she may lay her young."

"Dandelion seeds...": From Sachs's poem "This Land."

THE DON

Bobrowski first came across the River Don as a POW in central Russia in the late 1940s.

Div: An evil spirit, often appearing in the form of a bird. Plays an ominous role as a foreteller of ill fortune in *The Song of Prince Igor's Campaign*.

ICONS

Joanne: The twelfth-century Archbishop of Novgorod.

UNDER THE EDGE OF NIGHT

An early poem in Bobrowski's "landscapes-with-people" mode, composed in 1952, alongside his "Pruzzian Elegy."

NORTH RUSSIAN TOWN

Pustoshka: Town on the Velikaya River where Bobrowski was briefly stationed during World War II.

IN TRANSIT

Tolstoy: Unhappy with what he took to be his wife's materialistic possessiveness, in 1910 Tolstoy fled his family's estate at Yasnaya Polyana, later dying of heart failure at a railroad station in Astapovo.

ABOVE THE RIVER

The river is the Volkhov, flowing north from Lake Ilmen toward nearby Novgorod.

CATHEDRAL 1941

Sophia: In the summer of 1941, Bobrowski witnessed the extensive damage done to the eleventh-century Saint Sophia Cathedral in the ancient Novgorod Kremlin.

my eyes / still bright: See Psalm 13:3, "O Lord and God, lighten mine eyes, lest I sleep the sleep of death."

REPORT

Bajla Gelblung: After a photo and caption reproduced in Gerhard Schoenberner's 1960 study of the Shoah, *The Yellow Star.*

THE ROAD TO TOMSK

Czarist deportation route over the Urals to Siberia—to which, according to Bobrowski, a certain Yelizaveta (or Elizabeth) was sent.

RUSSIAN SONGS

Marina: Marina Mniszech, Polish-born noblewoman and tsarina of Russia during the early seventeenth-century Time of Troubles. Later imprisoned by Michael Romanov in a legendary tower on the Volga near Nizhny Novgorod.

IN MEMORY OF B.L.

The title masks the identity of Boris Leonidovich Pasternak, still a persona non grata in the GDR, having been forced to decline his 1958 Nobel by Soviet authorities. The poem was composed the day after Pasternak's death on May 30, 1960. Bobrowski later translated three of his love poems.

THE ROAD HOME

the house of old: Bobrowski's grandparents' house in Motzischken, on the Lithuanian right bank of the River Memel.

I shall make it / over the river: See Matthew 14:25ff.

ALWAYS TO BE NAMED

does their speech / move in the dark: See Psalm 19:2, "Day unto day uttereth speech and night unto night sheweth knowledge."

MICKIEWICZ

A dramatic monologue rehearsing familiar scenes from the life of the Polish Lithuanian national poet Adam Mickiewicz (1798–1855) —his student days in Vilna, his banishment to central Russia, his 1824 excursion to Crimea, his later émigré life in Paris and friendship with Chopin.

Weathersigns (1966)

J. S. BACH

that he saw / the bay: An early draft of the poem more explicitly evokes the twenty-year-old Bach's long trek to the Baltic coastal town of Lübeck in 1705 to visit the ailing sixty-eight-year-old Dieterich Buxtehude, the influence of whose melancholy compositions (or "Evening Music") continued to deepen during Bach's later residences in Anhalt-Köthen (1717–1723) and Leipzig (1723–1744).

(at 16'): The next-to-lowest pitch of an organ stop, sixteen feet in height.

THE FRIEND

the old man: See C. P. Cavafy's 1897 poem "An Old Man."

Euphronios: Ancient Greek vase painter and potter, known for his red-figure technique.

MOZART

Colloredo: The Archbishop Hieronymus, Count Colloredo of Salzburg, became Mozart's patron in 1772 when he was just sixteen. After years of spats, Mozart resigned from his employ in Vienna in 1781, later moving on to Prague.

Constanze: Mozart's wife, a soprano.

MIDSTREAM

No One: As Ulysses named himself in the cave of Polyphemus in Book 6 of the Odyssey. See also Celan's "No-One's-Rose."

MIDNIGHT VILLAGE

as Saturn's steps / grow near: Written a week after construction on the Berlin Wall began on August 13, 1961.

SHADOWLAND

Ragana: In Lithuanian and Latvian folklore, a Hecate-like witch associated with the moon and the underworld.

TO KLOPSTOCK

Bobrowski considered the poetry of Friedrich Gottlieb Klopstock (1724–1803) to be the "most significant event in German literature."

a shadow tale of guilt / and atonement: The redemption of mankind's sins through Christ is the central theme of Klopstock's 1773 Miltonic epic *The Messiah.*

VOLGA TOWNS

Minin: Kuzma Minin, folk hero, leader of the early seventeenth-century uprising in Nizhny Novgorod against the Polish-Lithuanian occupation of Russia during the Time of Troubles.

Stenka: Another folk hero, Cossack leader of the revolt against the nobility and tsarist bureaucracy of southern Russia in the later seventeenth century.

TO RUNGE

Philipp Otto Runge (1777–1810), a visionary German landscape painter, sometimes compared to Blake, born in Wolgast on the Baltic Sea (then still Swedish Pomerania). In his well-known *Self-Portrait* of 1810, he glances over his shoulder. Coins were traditionally placed in the mouths of the dying. Runge suffered from tuberculosis his entire life and died of it at age thirty-three.

WHEN THEY HAVE BEEN DESERTED

the thornbush: See Exodus 3:2.

yet I do not thirst: See John 4:14: "But whosoever drinketh of the water that I shall give him shall never thirst."

JAKUB BART IN RALBITZ

Jakub Bart-Ćišinski, major Sorbian nationalist writer of the late nineteenth century. The town of Ralbitz was located in Upper Lusatia (in Saxony), a central settlement area of the Sorbs—or the Wends—most of whom were engaged in the mining industry and whose native tongue was closely related to the Czech and Lechitic languages. The quotation toward the end of the poem is drawn from Bart-Ćišinski's poem "O tempora O mores." Sorbian was finally recognized as an official "minority language" of the GDR in 1977.

ARRIVAL

May evoke Bobrowski's arrival in East Berlin around Christmastime 1949, after his four and a half years spent in Soviet POW camps. The second, more paranoid 1963 section of the poem seems to suggest a presence in the attic, listening in (as in the film *The Lives of Others*).

ANSWER

This 1963 poem in the manner of Bobrowski's mentor Peter Huchel is thought to allude to the latter's official disgrace in 1962—which led to his ouster as the editor of the influential GDR cultural journal *Sinn und Form* and his subsequent house arrest and surveillance by the Stasi for the next nine years.

so that / the stone cry out: See Luke 19:39–40: "And some of the Pharisees from among the multitude said unto him, master, rebuke thy disciples. And he answered and said unto them, I tell you that, if these should hold their peace, the stones would immediately cry out."

BARLACH IN GÜSTROW

Ernst Barlach (1870–1938), a German expressionist sculptor, printmaker, and writer, whose work was later condemned by the Nazis as "degenerate art." Evokes a photograph taken of him late in life in Güstrow, in Western Pomerania, leaning on his cane.

J. M. R. LENZ

Livonian-born Jakob Michael Reinhold Lenz (1751–1792) studied in Königsberg, then moved to Strasbourg where he became Goethe's chum (who dubbed him "whimsical" and "adorable") and gained fame as the author of two experimental Sturm und Drang plays, *The Tutor* (1774) and *The Officers* (1776), revived by Bertolt Brecht's Berliner Ensemble in 1950. Having followed Goethe to the court of Weimar, Lenz was expelled by the latter for his "asininity" and, increasingly suffering from schizophrenia, entered the medical care of the social reformer and clergyman Johann Friedrich Oberlin in Alsace in early 1778—the subject of Georg Büchner's 1836 novella fragment *Lenz,* whose first sentence ("Lenz walked through the mountains") is quoted here (and by Celan at the outset of his 1960 "Meridian" speech). In 1779, still mentally unbalanced, Lenz joined his brother in Riga, before moving on to St. Petersburg. He was found dead in a Moscow street in June 1792.

NAMES FOR THE PERSECUTED

Old Prussian words: *gerwe* (crane), *angurys* (eel). See Bobrowski's earlier poem "Dead Language."

Holunder: See note to the poem "Elder Blossom."

TO JAWLENSKY

An ekphrastic tribute to the Russian German expressionist painter Alexej von Jawlensky (1864–1941), a member of Wassily Kandinsky's early Munich circle.

ESTHER

Adapted from Esther 1–7, the book in which the Jews of Persia, destined to be destroyed, are ultimately saved by Queen Esther—a miraculous rescue celebrated at Purim.

CITY

Those who called for your blood: From his office in the Union Verlag near Checkpoint Charlie, Bobrowski witnessed the death in August 1962 of the *Mauerspringer* Peter Fechter, a young construction worker who tried to flee across the Berlin Wall but who was shot dead by border guards while entangled in the barbed wire. One of his colleagues reported that Bobrowski showed him a poem referring to this event but that he later destroyed it and rewrote it into this more ironic, more cryptic lyric evoking a divided Berlin and the sodium-vapor lamps illuminating its wall.

KOLNO DANCE

Kolno: Town in Poland whose substantial Jewish community was destroyed by the Nazis in the early 1940s, here remembered as a *Totentanz*, or Dance of Death.

REAWAKENING

The title may also be translated as "resuscitation" or "resurrection." A pointed response to the nihilism of Celan's poem "Oben, geräuschlos" ("Above, noiseless") in his 1955 volume *Von Schwelle zu Schwelle* (*From Threshold to Threshold*), but never directly sent by Bobrowski to Celan in Paris in 1964, out of respect for the anguish the poet was then experiencing—the widow of the poet Yvan Goll having continued to publicly accuse him of having plagiarized her late husband's work.

white / with bones: See Ezekiel 37:1–5.

WITH THE SONGS OF SAPPHO

peplos: From a fragment of Sappho rediscovered on a scrap of papyrus in Berlin in 1896. Compare Ezra Pound's 1916 Sappho poem "Papyrus," which reads in its entirety: "Spring... / Too long... / Gongula..."

Solon: Legendary Athenian lawgiver, one of the Seven Sages of Greece.

OLD FARM IN HÄME

A record of Bobrowski's 1964 visit to Finland, where he met James Baldwin and discovered the poetry of Paavo Haavikko.

PRECAUTION

burdock: Traditional medicinal herb, renowned as a detoxifier of, among other things, the cirrhosis of the liver from which Bobrowski feared he suffered.

UNDINE

Ethereal water sprite, said to seek a human soul by marriage to a mortal yet risking death if betrayed. Subject of an Ingeborg Bachmann story that she offered to Bobrowski.

ALIENATION

Alternate title: "Estrangement."

ON CHRISTOPH MECKEL'S GRAPHIC WORKS

The poet and graphic artist Christoph Meckel (1935–2020) was one of Bobrowski's closest friends and designed several of his book covers.

TO HÖLTY

Ludwig Hölty (1748–1776), a German author of songs and ballads, and a disciple of Klopstock.

THE WORD "MAN" AS A TERM

Bobrowski's last published poem, written four months before his death. In the 1993 *Oxford English Dictionary*, the word "man" occurs between "mamzer" and "mana."

Unpublished Poems

PARTISAN WOODS

See chapter 7 of Timothy Snyder's *Bloodlands* for an account of partisan activity on the eastern front during World War II.

1943

In the spring of 1943, taking advantage of a brief military leave, Bobrowski returned to the small village of his childhood holidays (Motzischken in the Jura region) to marry Johanna Buddrus, who also had relatives in this area, and to whom this poem was dedicated in its manuscript version.

Later / I return. / I unlearn the dark: Most likely refers to Bobrowski's release in December 1949 from a Russian POW camp and his return to East Berlin.

TRAKL

Austrian Expressionist poet Georg Trakl (1887–1914), an important influence on Bobrowski, as these three imitations of his manner indicate.

TO * * *

The poem was privately sent to the East German poet Peter Jokostra (1912–2007), a friend of Celan's, whom Bobrowski first met in Berlin in February 1957, where they shared their wartime memories, including Jokostra's desertion from the German army during the siege of Moscow.

"Provençal Intermezzo": Title of a section Jokostra's 1958 volume of poetry, *Sun on the Wall*.

the Jewish girl: Wronka, Jokostra's former Polish girlfriend, was a music student in Poznan when the Germans invaded Poland in 1939. The Nazis killed her parents, but she managed to escape; she was captured and then murdered at Treblinka in mid-1942.

Raseiniai: See the poem "To the Jewish Peddler A.S."

the river flowed around the mountain: The River Memel, or Nemunas, as it courses around the sacred Lithuanian mountain of the gods, the Rombinus.

the weathered god of the fields: The old Baltic fertility god Patrimpas, or Potrimpos.

IN MEMORY OF HÖLDERLIN

Oka: A river in central Russia, the largest right tributary of the Volga.

Klyazma: Left tributary of the Oka.

Neri: A river that rises in Belarus and flows through Vilna.

Vladimir: A city east of Moscow located on the Klyazma River.

"Go and greet / the sweet Garonne": An ecstatic imperative lifted from Hölderlin's poem "Andenken" ("Remembrance").

RABELAIS

Thélème: Fictional abbey in Rabelais's *Gargantua* and *Pantagruel*, whose Utopian motto was *"Fay ce que vouldras"* ("Do what you will").

ROSA LUXEMBURG

Polish-born Jewish activist Rosa Luxemburg (1871–1919) was a Marxist theorist and revolutionary leader of the Spartacus League during the German Revolution of 1918–1919. The poem is based on her *Letters from Prison* (1922), in which she frequently speaks of hearing birds over the course of her confinement.

STAND. SPEAK.

Nineveh: See Jonah 3:1–10.

WAILING WALL

Daniel stood at the Wall: See Daniel 5:24–31.

FRAGMENTS

These three late fragments were discovered in a pocket notebook.

DANTE ALIGHIERI The New Life
Translated by Dante Gabriel Rossetti; Preface by Michael Palmer

KINGSLEY AMIS Collected Poems: 1944–1979

YURI ANDRUKHOVYCH Set Change
Translated by Ostap Kin and John Hennessy

ANTONELLA ANEDDA Historiae
Translated by Patrizio Ceccagnoli and Susan Stewart

GUILLAUME APOLLINAIRE Zone: Selected Poems
Translated by Ron Padgett

AUSTERITY MEASURES The New Greek Poetry
Edited by Karen Van Dyck

CHARLES BAUDELAIRE Flowers of Evil
Translated by George Dillon and Edna St. Vincent Millay

HAYIM NAHMAN BIALIK On the Slaughter
Translated and with an introduction by Peter Cole

JOHANNES BOBROWSKI Under the Edge of Night
Translated by Richard Sieburth

SZILÁRD BORBÉLY Berlin-Hamlet
Translated by Ottilie Mulzet

SZILÁRD BORBÉLY In a Bucolic Land
Translated by Ottilie Mulzet

ANDRÉ BRETON AND PHILIPPE SOUPAULT
The Magnetic Fields
Translated by Charlotte Mandel

MARGARET CAVENDISH *Edited by Michael Robbins*

PAUL CELAN LETTERS TO GISÈLE
Translated by Jason Kavett

AMIT CHAUDHURI SWEET SHOP: NEW AND SELECTED POEMS, 1985–2023

NAJWAN DARWISH EXHAUSTED ON THE CROSS
Translated by Kareem James Abu-Zeid; Foreword by Raúl Zurita

NAJWAN DARWISH NOTHING MORE TO LOSE
Translated by Kareem James Abu-Zeid

FARNOOSH FATHI GRANNY CLOUD

BENJAMIN FONDANE CINEPOEMS AND OTHERS
Edited by Leonard Schwartz

GLORIA GERVITZ MIGRATIONS: POEM, 1976–2020
Translated by Mark Schafer

ZUZANNA GINCZANKA FIREBIRD
Translated by Alissa Valles

PERE GIMFERRER *Translated by Adrian Nathan West*

W. S. GRAHAM *Selected by Michael Hofmann*

SAKUTARŌ HAGIWARA CAT TOWN
Translated by Hiroaki Sato

MICHAEL HELLER TELESCOPE: SELECTED POEMS

MIGUEL HERNÁNDEZ *Selected and translated by Don Share*

EMMANUEL HOCQUARD ELEGIES
Translated by Cole Swensen

RICHARD HOWARD RH ♥ HJ AND OTHER AMERICAN WRITERS
Introduction by Timothy Donnelly

RYSZARD KRYNICKI OUR LIFE GROWS
Translated by Alissa Valles; Introduction by Adam Michnik

LOUISE LABÉ LOVE SONNETS AND ELEGIES
Translated by Richard Sieburth

V. R. "BUNNY" LANG THE MIRACULOUS SEASON
Edited by Rosa Campbell

LI SHANGYIN *Edited and translated by Chloe Garcia Roberts*

AT THE LOUVRE POEMS BY 100 CONTEMPORARY WORLD POETS

OSIP MANDELSTAM VORONEZH NOTEBOOKS
Translated by Andrew Davis

ARVIND KRISHNA MEHROTRA *Selected by Vidyan Ravinthiran; Introduction by Amit Chaudhuri*

HENRI MICHAUX A CERTAIN PLUME
Translated by Richard Sieburth; Preface by Lawrence Durrell

MELISSA MONROE MEDUSA BEACH

EUGENIO MONTALE LATE MONTALE
Selected and translated by George Bradley

CHRISTIAN MORGENSTERN THE GALLOWS SONGS
Translated by Max Knight; Introduction by Samuel Titan

JOAN MURRAY DRAFTS, FRAGMENTS, AND POEMS: THE COMPLETE POETRY
Edited and with an introduction by Farnoosh Fathi; Preface by John Ashbery

ÁLVARO MUTIS MAQROLL'S PRAYER AND OTHER POEMS
Translated by Chris Andrews, Edith Grossman, and Alastair Reid

VIVEK NARAYANAN AFTER

SILVINA OCAMPO *Selected and translated by Jason Weiss*

EUGENE OSTASHEVSKY THE FEELING SONNETS

EUGENE OSTASHEVSKY The Pirate Who Does Not Know the Value of Pi
Art by Eugene and Anne Timerman

ELISE PARTRIDGE The If Borderlands: Collected Poems

CESARE PAVESE Hard Labor
Translated by William Arrowsmith; afterword by Ted Olson

DAVID PLANTE The Death of a Greek Lover

VASKO POPA *Selected and translated by Charles Simic*

J.H. PRYNNE The White Stones
Introduction by Peter Gizzi

ALICE PAALEN RAHON Shapeshifter
Translated and with an introduction by Mary Ann Caws

A.K. RAMANUJAN The Interior Landscape: Classical Tamil Love Poems

PIERRE REVERDY *Edited by Mary Ann Caws*

DENISE RILEY Say Something Back & Time Lived, Without Its Flow

ARTHUR RIMBAUD The Drunken Boat: Selected Writings
Edited by Mark Polizzotti

STEPHEN RODEFER Four Lectures

AMELIA ROSSELLI Sleep

JACK SPICER After Lorca
Preface by Peter Gizzi

THE TEN THOUSAND LEAVES Poems from the Man'yōshū
Translated by Ian Hideo Levy

MARINA TSVETAEVA Three by Tsvetaeva
Translated by Andrew Davis

CÉSAR VALLEJO, TRILCE
Translated and with glosses by William Rowe and Helen Dimos

ALEXANDER VVEDENSKY AN INVITATION FOR ME TO THINK
Translated by Eugene Ostashevsky and Matvei Yankelevich

WANG YIN A SUMMER DAY IN THE COMPANY OF GHOSTS
Translated by Andrea Lingenfelter

WALT WHITMAN DRUM-TAPS: THE COMPLETE 1865 EDITION
Edited by Lawrence Kramer

NACHOEM M. WIJNBERG *Translated by David Colmer*

LAKDHAS WIKKRAMASINHA
Edited by Michael Ondaatje and Aparna Halpé

ELIZABETH WILLIS ALIVE: NEW AND SELECTED POEMS

ZHENG XIAOQIONG IN THE ROAR OF THE MACHINE
Translated by Eleanor Goodman

RAÚL ZURITA INRI
Translated by William Rowe; Preface by Norma Cole